LA VIDA TAPA

EL TAPEO ES LIBER TAD

Esto no es un bar de tapas

TICKETS

Tapejar és compartir

LA VIDA TAPA

TICKETS

TAPAS ARE FREE DOM

THIS IS NOT A TAPAS BAR

LA VIDA TAPA

ETS

LES TAPES SÓN LLIBER TAT

LES TAPES SÓN LLIBER TAT

TICKETS

Tapear es compartir

LA VIDA TAPA

TAPAS ARE FREE DOM

THIS IS NOT A TAPAS BAR

TICKETS

TICKETS

LA VIDA TAPA

LA VIDA TAPA

Això no és pas un bar de tapes

Esto no es un bar de tapas

EL TAPEO ES LIBER TAD

EL TAPEO ES LIBER TAD

Tapear es compartir

Això no és pas un bar de tapes

LES TAPES SÓN LLIBER TAT

La vida tapa

TICKETS

TICKETS

TAPAS ARE FREE DOM

TAPEJAR ÉS COMPARTIR

TICKETS

THIS IS NOT A TAPAS BAR

THIS IS NOT A TAPAS BAR

LES TAPES SÓN LLIBER TAT

TICKETS

TAPEAR ES COMPARTIR

La vida tapa

LA VIDA TAPA

LA VIDA TAPA

Tapas are free dom

TICKETS

LA VIDA TAPA

Això no és pas un bar de tapes

TICKETS

Tapejar és compartir

EL TAPEO ES LIBER TAD

LA VIDA TAPA

TAPAS

TICKETS CUISINE

Original title: Tapas. La cocina del Tickets

First edition: July 2014
Second edition: March 2016

Avda. Diagonal, 189 – 08018 Barcelona
www.rbalibros.com

Gastronomic coordination: Miguel Estrada Domínguez
Recipes and texts: Albert Adrià Acosta
English translation review: Tristán Steward
Translation: textosBCN (Maria Friel), for Bonalletra Alcompas
Proofreading: textosBCN (Dustin Langan), for Bonalletra Alcompas
Graphic design: Compañía
Editorial production: Bonalletra Alcompas

Ref.: RPRA187
ISBN: 978-84-9056-301-4
Legal deposit: B. 15.887-2014

ALBERT ADRIÀ

TAPAS

TICKETS CUISINE

RBA

TICKETS

“For us, La vida tapa is a global concept which links gastronomy to a way of understanding life: an amusing way of eating that turns the diner into a performer in a play, a chorus magazine or a Vaudeville variety show, into the leading character of a singing, comic theatrical performance. It is a staging of real life. At La vida tapa, there’s no place for boredom, sorrow or loneliness, but plenty of room for laughter, sharing and good company.”

ALBERT ADRIÀ

S
TICKETS
TICKETS
LOS CAFÈS LAVAZZA
COCA COLA
VIDA TAPA
LA VIDA TAPA
LA VIDA TAPA

CONTENTS

TICKETS: TAPAS...

& FIESTA

Some people might think that it's a tad hasty to write a book about a restaurant that is barely three years old. Nevertheless, I believe you should write a book when you have something to say. And after the first three intense years at Tickets, I feel that I have something to say now. I admit that there is also a selfish motive behind this book, since putting together Tapas has been a self-help exercise for me, forcing me to analyse and reflect upon my work. I've realised that I like to reaffirm myself in culinary parameters that continually evolve, just as I do.

IN SEARCH OF ENTERTAINMENT

The origin of Tickets dates back five years. Back then, night after night, on leaving the Inopia Clàssic Bar, a traditional tapas bar in Barcelona I co-ran until 2009, I drove down the street Tamarit and, at the intersection with Entença, I would see the premises of a former car dealership for rent. Every time I came across this corner, I couldn't help but imagine the possibilities a premises of these characteristics could offer me, particularly since one of Inopia's problems was the limited space. But, then again, I hadn't planned to set up another business: I knew that the closing of elBulli was imminent, as well as the end of my tenure as partner at Inopia, and I felt it was time to indulge in some well-deserved holidays after twenty-three years of uninterrupted work.

It was all to change on 2 February 2010. We were enjoying a family celebration to mark my son Àlex's third birthday in the restaurant Rías de Galicia, one of our favourite eateries. Shortly before the cake, Juan Carlos Iglesias, the first born of the family who own the establishment, jovially informed us that my premises, the space I dreamed about every night, was within reach and that, if we played the game, they'd join in too. No sooner said than done, we set up a company between the three Iglesias brothers, Ferran and myself, and we got down to work on designing a tapas bar, which still didn't have a name at that point…

BUILDING THE CULINARY CONCEPT

Prior to opening, we organised two Tickets workshops, one in elBulli, involving my brother Ferran, Oriol Castro and Eduard Xatruch, and another in our workshop on the street Portaferrissa in Barcelona, with Andrés Conde, Miguel Estrada and myself. After two months of working separately, we met up in elBulli to build a general consensus and, two weeks later, we prepared a meal for the Iglesias and Adrià brothers in the workshop, during which we served almost forty dishes. That is how the first Tickets menu came about and it already pointed in a clear direction: on the one hand, tipping its hat to elBulli, with spherical olives and airbags, our signature inflated bread rolls; and on the other hand, there was already a sense of a new culinary language, featuring oysters, cod ratatouille and an orange and olive salad.

Though it was clear to me that I did not want to exploit direct references to our previous work, at first I had no choice. I wanted to stir my memories in the most primitive and instinctive way possible. After all, the most important thing was the storyline, the style, and establishing a yardstick that drew the boundaries: between dishes in the first menu, the tuna belly tartar served with Piparra chili pepper jus and apple meringue could be at one end and, at the other end of the scale, rabbit ribs with garlic mayonnaise, a dish I took with me from Inopia and used as a resource.

A NEIGHBOURHOOD BULLI

We hadn't even opened Tickets yet and were in the testing phase when a customer raised their hand to catch my attention. Arriving at his table, he proclaimed, "Hey, Albert, how funny! It's like a neighbourhood elBulli!". Soon after, another customer opened the menu and asked me, "Excuse me, what do you have here from elBulli? Because I've never been, you know?". This curtain raiser steered me in the direction of where the Tickets concept was heading, already moving away from the "bar" concept we had initially planned (we had even registered the brand ticketsbar.es, but the direction had changed). The following few weeks were really intense as we began to define our identity with two clear goals in mind: **fun** (we're constantly told we achieve this) and **nurturing contact** with the customers (it's really direct, we work and move amongst them). It is ultimately them who instinctively and effectively guided us towards the sought-after style.

Today we have a fully trained and motivated team, who are going from strength to strength. Thanks to their energy, we have been able to come up with some 250 recipes, not to mention the superb work we have undertaken in the realm of sweet dishes, an effort I hope will be rewarded with another book. But that's another story.

Call in, see for yourself and enjoy...

Albert Adrià

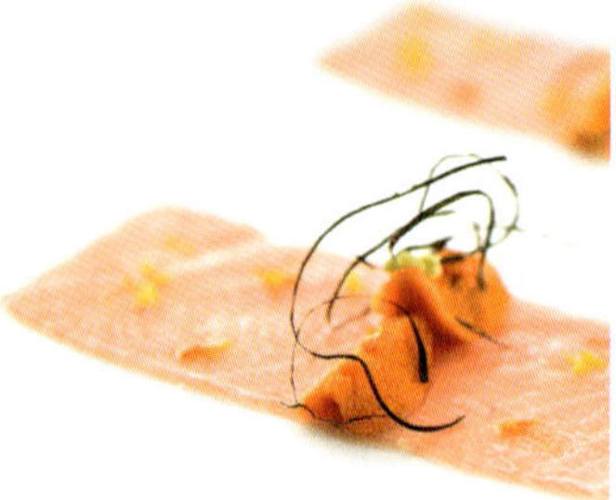

EL PICOTEO

TICKETS OLIVES, VERDIAL VARIETY

X 4

1 For the olive juice
450 g Verdial unpitted olives

2 For the spherical olive base
200 g Verdial olive juice
(see point 1)
1.2 g calcium salt (Calcic)
0.7 g xanthan

3 For the flavoured olive oil
20 g garlic
400 g virgin olive oil
¼ sprig thyme
¼ sprig rosemary
1 lemon
1 orange
2.5 g black peppercorns

4 For the alginate bath
500 g mineral water
2.5 g alginate (Algin)

5 For the Verdial olives
q.s. alginate bath *(see point 4)*
q.s. spherical olive base
(see point 2)
q.s. flavoured olive oil
(see point 3)
q.s. mineral water

❶ For the Verdial olive juice

See next page.

❷ For the spherical olive base

Combine the olive juice and Calcic and blend in a mixer to dissolve. Add the xanthan and blend again until smooth. Let the mixture stand in the fridge for 24 h to eliminate the air bubbles. To speed up the process, a vacuum-sealing machine may be used.
Strain the mixture. Store in a container and refrigerate.

❸ For the flavoured olive oil

Open the head of garlic to extract the whole cloves with the skin intact.
Put them unpeeled in a saucepan with 100 g of virgin olive oil, and sauté at 70ºC for 1 hour. Allow to cool to room temperature. Add the remainder of the oil, thyme, rosemary, orange and lemon peel and black pepper. Set aside.

❹ For the alginate bath

Mix the water and the alginate in a mixer until fully dissolved, then strain. Let the mixture stand for 24 h in a bowl in the fridge to eliminate the accumulated air bubbles; alternatively, speed up the process in a vacuum-sealing machine.
Keep refrigerated.

❺ For the Verdial olives

Put the alginate bath in a container, to a height of 5 cm approx.
Fill a 5-ml spherical spoon with the spherical olive base and pour the mixture into the alginate bath to form spherical olives.
Cook in the alginate bath for 1 min.
Remove the olive with a slotted spoon and rinse with water.
Put the olives in a bowl with the flavoured olive oil.
Store in the fridge.

Finishing and presentation

Fill each jar with flavoured oil to a height of 4 cm. Place 6 spherical olives in each one using a slotted spoon.
Serve the olives together with a slotted spoon at the tableside.

HOW TO PREPARE OLIVE JUICE

Besides preparing the Tickets olives, olive juice can be used as a sauce in many other dishes, such as salads, jellies and cocktails. If you do not have a vacuum-sealing machine to prepare this dish, *see page 170*.

Drain the olives from the jar, discarding the marinade of pepper, garlic and spices.

1

Pitt the olives. If you have an olive pitter, the operation is faster. Discard the pits.

2

Purée the olive flesh with a hand mixer.

3

Strain this purée through a fine sieve (Superbag). Place in a vacuum bag, remove the air and keep refrigerated.

4

TICKETS OLIVES, GORDAL VARIETY

X 4

❶ For the olive juice
450 g Gordal unpitted olives

❷ For the spherical olive base
200 g Gordal olive juice
(see page 17)
1.2 g calcium salt (Calcic)
0.7 g xanthan

❸ For the alginate bath
500 g mineral water
2.5 g alginate (Algin)

❹ For the Gordal olives
q.s. alginate bath *(see point 3)*
q.s. spherical olive base
(see point 2)
q.s. olive oil, 0.4° acidity
q.s. mineral water

Finishing and presentation
400 g olive oil, 0.4° acidity
10 g cinnamon stick
1 star anise
1 lemon

❶ For the olive juice
See page 17.

❷ For the spherical olive base
See point 2 on page 16.

❸ For the alginate bath
Mix the water and the alginate in a mixer until fully dissolved, then strain.
Let the mixture stand for 24 h in a bowl in the fridge to eliminate the accumulated air bubbles; alternatively, speed up the process in a vacuum-sealing machine.

❹ For the Gordal olives
Put the alginate bath in a container, to a height of 5 cm approx.
Fill a 5-ml spherical spoon to the top with the spherical olive base and pour the mixture into the alginate bath to form spherical olives. Cook in the alginate bath for 1 min.
Remove from the alginate bath with a slotted spoon and rinse with water.
Put the olives in a bowl with the olive oil, 0.4° acidity.
Store in the fridge.

Finishing and presentation
Break the cinnamon sticks into 2-cm pieces. One piece is needed per jar.
Break the star anise into 4 pieces.
Using a zester or paring knife, peel off the coloured part of the lemon rind. One piece of peel is needed per jar.
Fill each jar with olive oil, 0.4° acidity, to a height of 4 cm.
Place 6 spherical olives in each one using a slotted spoon. Put 1 piece of lemon peel, 1 piece of cinnamon and 1 piece of star anise in each jar.
Serve the olives together with a slotted spoon at the tableside.

SANGRÍA-INFUSED WATERMELON

X 4

1. **For the syrup**
60 g sugar
60 g mineral water

2. **For the sangría**
110 g syrup *(see point 1)*
240 g red wine
65 g Grand Marnier
55 g brandy
40 g orange juice

3. **For the watermelon cubes**
2 kg seedless watermelon

4. **To infuse the watermelon cubes**
¼ bunch fresh mint
1 cinnamon stick
1 sweet orange

Finishing and presentation
1.2 kg crushed ice
1 lemon
1 orange
16 Atsina cress sprouts
16 mint leaves

❶ For the syrup
Mix the water and sugar in a pan. Bring to the boil to dissolve the sugar. Set aside.

❷ For the sangría
Mix all the cold ingredients in a bowl. Set aside.

❸ For the watermelon cubes
See next page.

❹ To infuse the watermelon cubes
See next page.

Finishing and presentation
Open the vacuum bag and remove the watermelon cubes.
Cut the orange peel into julienne strips 1 mm thick and break the cinnamon stick into 8-cm pieces.
Serve the watermelon in glass bottles cut in half horizontally; on a bed of crushed ice, arrange 7 watermelon cubes on each one.
Top the cubes with two strips of orange peel and 2 pieces of cinnamon.
Grate orange and lemon zest over the watermelon.
Garnish with 4 mint leaves and 4 Atsina sprouts.

Cut the watermelon into 2-cm slices.

1

Make 2-cm cubes, discarding the softest or unripe ones and any white seeds.

2

THE INFUSION TECHNIQUE

This method involves immersing the food in a liquid and vacuum-sealing it. The air trapped inside the food pores can therefore be removed, and when the vacuum seal is broken, these spaces are filled with the liquid in which the food was immersed, thereby changing its original colour, flavour and aroma. If you do not have a vacuum-sealing machine, *see page 170*.

Put 7 watermelon cubes, 1 cinnamon stick, 2 sprigs of fresh mint and 2 pieces of orange peel in each vacuum bag.

3

Fill 3 additional bags with the same ingredients. Add the sangría.

4

Place each bag in a vacuum-sealing machine and apply 100%.

5

Set aside for at least 2 h in a bowl of iced water in the fridge.

6

LA VIDA

IBERIAN TUNA HAM

X 4

❶ **To clean and cut the tuna belly**
1 kg tuna belly
(minimum quantity for a good result)

❷ **For the ham fat**
100 g Iberian ham fat
20 g olive oil, 0.4° acidity
10 g mineral water

❸ **For the crushed pine nuts**
20 g wild untoasted pine nuts

Finishing and presentation
16 grissini bread sticks
q.s. Guérande grey salt
q.s. black pepper

❶ To clean and cut the tuna belly

With a sharp knife, remove the upper tissue of the tuna belly and the skin, taking care not to cut the white fat found between the skin and the flesh (which will give the appearance of cured ham fat).
Next, remove the bones from the tuna belly, going over it well with a sharp knife so as not to waste any meat.
Divide the tuna belly: use the top part in one piece to make the dish and set aside the bottom part for other dishes.
Cut the tuna belly into pieces 6 cm long x 12 cm wide. The length will depend on the tuna belly. (This is an approximate size that acts as a guideline to take full advantage of the piece.)
Cover the piece with plastic wrap and freeze.

❷ For the ham fat

Remove any rancid parts from the pieces of ham and cut into 1-cm pieces.
Mix the ham fat, the olive oil and the water in a pan.
Cook on a low heat until the water has fully evaporated and the fat has melted, without allowing it to fry.
Strain, set the ham fat aside in a bowl and refrigerate.

❸ For the crushed wild pine nuts

Using a knife, break the pine nuts into three pieces. Set aside.

Finishing and presentation

Thirty min before serving the dish, remove the cured ham fat from the fridge. Using a meat-slicing machine, cut the block of frozen tuna into thin slices 0.2 cm thick. Arrange the tuna slices on the parchment paper in a line and slightly overlapping, so that the top part of the tuna with the fat is visible. Each person will be served a 40 g portion of tuna belly (5 slices approx.).
Using a brush, paint the slices with the ham fat.
Put 4 grains of grey salt in the centre of each tuna belly slice.
Sprinkle black pepper and a few pieces of pine nut on top of the salt.
Put the tuna belly under the grill for 2 sec to warm it lightly and make the ham fat sweat. Serve on a platter and garnish each portion with 4 grissini bread sticks.

THIN LAYERS OF TUNA BELLY WITH SEA URCHINS, GINGER AND YUZU

X 4

1 To clean and cut the tuna belly
1 kg tuna belly
(minimum quantity for a good result)

2 For the nori seaweed strips
1 strip nori seaweed, 20 x 20 cm

3 To clean the sea urchin roe
400 g sea urchins
(40 g clean sea urchin roe)
50 g mineral water
q.s. fine salt

4 For the grated ginger
5 g fresh ginger

5 For the soy sauce
100 g soy sauce
0.4 g xanthan

6 For the grated wasabi
q.s. grated wasabi paste

Finishing and presentation
1 yuzu
q.s. fine salt

1 To clean and cut the tuna belly
With a sharp knife, remove the upper tissue of the tuna belly and the skin, taking care not to cut the white fat found between the skin and the flesh (which will give the appearance of cured ham fat).
Next, remove the bones from the tuna belly, going over it well with a sharp knife so as not to waste any meat. Divide the tuna belly: use the top part in one piece for this dish and set aside the bottom part for other dishes.
Cut the tuna belly into pieces 6 cm long x 12 cm wide. The length will depend on the tuna belly. (This is an approximate size that acts as a guideline to take full advantage of the piece.)
Cover the piece with plastic wrap and freeze.

2 For the nori seaweed strips
Using a paper cutter or knife, cut the nori seaweed into fine strips 2 mm wide x 3 cm long; then set aside in a bowl.

3 To clean the sea urchin roe
Open the sea urchins at the base using scissors, making a circle 2 cm in diameter. Remove the roe from the sea urchins and rinse in a bath of water and salt to remove any impurities.
Dry on a paper towel and store in a container in the fridge.

4 For the grated ginger
Peel the ginger using a peeler. Grate and store in a small plastic cup covered with a damp paper towel in the fridge.

5 For the soy sauce
Mix half the soy sauce with the xanthan.
Remove the air in a vacuum-sealing machine and add the remaining soy sauce. Set aside in the fridge. If you do not have a vacuum-sealing machine, *see page 170*.

6 For the grated wasabi
Put the grated wasabi into a piping bag and set aside.

Finishing and presentation

Using a meat-slicing machine, cut the block of frozen tuna into thin layers 2 mm thick.
Arrange 4 separate layers of tuna on top of parchment paper.
Season with salt, grate the yuzu using a grater (Microplane) over the tuna belly and place a dab of grated ginger on the upper left-hand side of each layer.
Place 2 pieces of sea urchin roe in the centre of each layer, and season with salt. Put a dab of soy sauce on each corner of the layer. Just before serving, put a pinch of grated wasabi and 4 nori seaweed strips on top of the sea urchin roe.

AIR-BAGUETTE WRAPPED IN IBERIAN HAM

X 4

1 For the air-baguette dough
340 g soft flour
12 g compressed fresh yeast
200 g full-fat milk
4 g fine salt

2 For the air-baguettes
300 g air-baguette dough
(see point 1)
q.s. all-purpose flour

3 For the ham fat
50 g ham fat
10 g olive oil, 0.4° acidity
5 g mineral water

4 For the slices of cured ham
500 g whole and boneless
Iberian ham (Joselito)

1 For the air-baguette dough
Pour the flour and the crumbled yeast into a kneading machine or food processor and knead at minimum speed.
Gradually add the milk and mix for 6 min.
Add the salt and mix for an additional 6 min, until it is well kneaded.
Set the well-covered dough aside in a bowl in the fridge for 24 h.

2 For the air-baguettes
Prepare 75-g portions of dough and stretch into sheets in the pasta machine to a thickness of 2 mm approx. Arrange them on baking parchment. Cut the dough using a stainless steel mould in the shape of a baguette and place on a tray lined with baking parchment. Bake at 240°C (in the case of a steam oven, at 40% humidity) on an iron plate, until the air-baguettes are puffy and evenly golden, turning them over halfway through baking so that they are golden on both sides.
Allow to cool to room temperature and store in a container.

3 For the ham fat
Remove any rancid parts from the pieces of ham fat and cut into 1-cm pieces.
Mix the clean and chopped ham fat, the olive oil and the water in a pan.
Cook on a low heat until the water has fully evaporated and the fat has melted, without allowing it to fry. Strain the Iberian ham fat into a container and refrigerate.

4 For the slices of cured ham
Store the cured ham in the fridge for 24 h.
Dice the ham, which contains part fat and part tender meat, into chunks 9 cm long x 4 cm wide.
Thinly slice the chunks.
Cut four sheets of baking parchment into 12 x 8 cm pieces.
Brush them lightly with ham fat.
Arrange 3 slices of cured ham on each sheet of parchment, with the fat towards the left-hand side, starting from right to left.
Brush the slices with ham fat and cover them with another sheet of parchment.
Set aside in the fridge.

Finishing and presentation

Arrange the cured ham horizontally.
Place the air-baguette in the centre of the cured ham and, with the help of a palette knife, wrap it in the ham so that it adheres well.
Brush the air-baguette with the ham fat.

COD FRITTERS WITH PARSLEY POWDER

X 4

1 For the cod fritter tempura
130 g mineral water
10 g compressed fresh yeast
110 g all-purpose flour
10 g Trisol
3 g fine salt
3 g granulated sugar

2 For the parsley powder
50 g parsley

3 For the garlic oil
50 g olive oil, 0.4° acidity
15 g garlic

4 For the cod fritter batter
250 g desalted cod tail
1 kg mineral water
200 g Mona Lisa potatoes
45 g garlic oil *(see point 3)*
30 g pasteurised egg yolk
30 g cream, 35% fat
10 g garlic
q.s. salt and pepper

5 For the half-spheres of cod fritter batter
240 g cod fritter batter *(see point 4)*
50 g desalted cod tail
16 raw and peeled pine nuts

Finishing and presentation
100 g all-purpose flour
500 g olive oil, 0.4° acidity

❶ For the cod fritter tempura

Heat half the water, without letting it rise to 40°C, and mix with the yeast.
Add the flour, the Trisol and the remaining water and gradually mix with a whisk until smooth. Finally, add the sugar and salt, and mix.
Wrap the tempura in plastic wrap and let it ferment in the fridge for 12 h.

❷ For the parsley powder

Remove the leaves from the parsley and spread on a tray lined with baking parchment. Dry in the dehydrator at 45°C for 24 h. Dehydration can also be carried out in an oven. Grind with a grinder until 10 g of parsley powder is obtained. Set aside in a bowl.

❸ For the garlic oil

Crush the whole unpeeled garlic cloves to release their flavour. Sauté the oil and the garlic on a low heat for 10 min until the garlic has softened. Let it cool to room temperature and strain.
Set aside.

❹ For the cod fritter batter

Remove the bones from the cod tail using tweezers. Put the water, potatoes and garlic, both unpeeled, in a saucepan and cook until the potato has softened.
Remove the potato and the garlic from the water; then add the cod tails to the water, off the heat. Leave for 8 min in the hot water, stirring occasionally so that they cook on both sides. Peel the potatoes and the garlic while still hot and put in the food processor with the cod tails and the cream. Mix at speed 6 for 1 min. Run the food processor at speed 3 and add the egg yolk. Mix well and gradually add the garlic oil in a threadlike stream.
Add salt and pepper as necessary, wrap in plastic wrap and set aside in a bowl, letting it cool to room temperature.

❺ For the half-spheres of cod fritter batter

Dice the cod tail into 16 cubes, 5 x 5 mm.
Mix the fritter batter with a spatula and put in a piping bag. To shape the cod fritters, *see next page*.

Finishing and presentation

Once the fritters have been fried, drain on paper towels and sprinkle with parsley powder. Serve 3 or 4 fritters per portion.

PERFECT COD FRITTERS

This simple trick makes for uniform fritters both in shape and texture. A tapa full of contrast owing to the creaminess of the cod on the inside and the crispy tempura on the outside.

Fill a silicone mould with 16 half-spheres, 3 cm in diameter x 2 cm deep, with the cod fritter batter halfway. 1

Place a pine nut and a cube of cod on top; then cover with the batter. The result is 16 half-spheres, each weighing 18 g. Cover with plastic wrap and freeze for 12 h. 2

Remove from the mould while still frozen and store in a container. Set aside in the fridge for 2 h. 3

Dust the balls of batter with flour and dip in the tempura. Remove the cod fritters with a fork, drain slightly and fry in oil at 190ºC, turning them over until golden. 4

MINI AIRBAGS FILLED WITH MANCHEGO CHEESE *ESPUMA*

X 4

❶ **For the mini-airbag dough**
340 g all-purpose flour
12 g compressed fresh yeast
200 g full-fat milk
4 g fine salt

❷ **For the mini airbags**
q.s. mini-airbag dough
(see point 1)

❸ **To pierce the mini airbags**
25 mini airbags *(see point 2)*

❹ **For the cheese *espuma* (light mousse)**
100 g Manchego cheese
500 g cream, 35% fat
2 g fine salt

❺ **For the cheese shavings**
q.s. Manchego cheese

Finishing and presentation
30 g hazelnut oil caviar (Caviaroli)
q.s toasted hazelnut skins
q.s. coarse salt
q.s. lemon thyme

❶ For the mini-airbag dough

Pour the flour and the crumbled yeast into a kneading machine or food processor with the dough hook and knead at minimum speed.
Gradually add the milk and mix for 6 min.
Add the salt and mix for an additional 6 min, until it is well kneaded. Set the well-covered dough aside in a bowl in the fridge for 24 h.

❷ For the mini airbags

See next page, from points 1 to 5.

❸ To pierce the mini airbags

See next page, point 6.

❹ For the cheese *espuma*

Remove the cheese rind and cut the cheese into small 5-mm pieces.
Heat the cream, and when it is on the verge of boiling, beat it with the cheese in a mixer to a fine cream.
Add salt as necessary, strain and pour into a half-litre siphon. Close and charge with two N_2O cartridges.
Let it cool in the fridge for 2 h.

❺ For the cheese shavings

Using a vegetable peeler, make 25 thin cheese shavings, 1 mm thick and 3 x 3 cm wide.
Place them on top of baking parchment and store in a container in the fridge.

Finishing and presentation

Put coarse salt on the dish to hold the mini airbags in place.
Fill each mini airbag with the cheese espuma.
Top the mini airbags with a cheese shaving.
Garnish each cheese shaving with the hazelnut oil caviar, the hazelnut skin and a sprig of lemon thyme. Arrange on a plate and serve.

MINI-AIRBAG RECIPE

This was one of elBulli's signature recipes and also is today at Tickets. This spectacular bread comes from a traditional Italian recipe. The result is a really light bread that is hollow on the inside.

Make dough portions of 90 g approx.

1

Stretch the dough into sheets in a pasta machine to a thickness of 2 mm approx. Arrange them on baking parchment.

2

Cut the dough using a circular mould 4.5 cm in diameter, and place the dough on a baking tray lined with parchment.

3

Bake at 240ºC (in the case of a steam oven, at 40% humidity) on an iron plate, until they are puffy and evenly golden.

4

Let the mini airbags cool to room temperature.

5

Using a drill and a thin bit, pierce the airbags to make a circular hole, 0.5 cm in diameter, in the top. Store the pierced airbags in a container.

6

1'40" QUAIL EGGS IN A NEST WITH ALMOGROTE-STYLE *MIGAS*

X 4

1 For the red mojo sauce
50 g Canarian red pepper (or the flesh of ñora peppers)
12 g white wine vinegar
6 g garlic
2 g black peppercorns
2 g dried cumin
2 g fine salt
100 g olive oil, 0.4° acidity

2 For the coarse *migas*
40 g lightly cured sheep's milk cheese
200 g Japanese breadcrumbs (Panko)
140 g red mojo sauce *(see point 1)*
4 g fine salt

3 To cook the eggs
16 quail eggs
200 g mineral water
6 g white wine vinegar
3 g fine salt
q.s. olive oil, 0.4° acidity (or red mojo oil, *see point 1*)

4 For the fine *migas*
25 g lightly cured sheep's milk cheese
100 g breadcrumbs
60 g red mojo sauce *(see point 1)*
4 g fine salt

Finishing and presentation
q.s. grey salt

❶ For the red mojo sauce

Blend all the ingredients together to a very fine texture. Allow to stand at room temperature for 3 h and remove the oil from the top.
Set the mojo oil aside separately, in the fridge.

❷ For the coarse *migas*

Grate the cheese with a grater. Hand mix the cheese with the remaining ingredients, obtaining a homogeneous mixture but allowing the Japanese breadcrumbs to retain their texture.
Bake in the oven for 15 min at 150°C and turn every 5 min to brown them on both sides.
Let them cool to room temperature and store in a container.

❸ To cook the eggs

See next page.

❹ For the fine *migas*

Grate the cheese with a grater. Mix all the ingredients together. Bake in the oven for 15 min at 150°C and stir every 5 min to brown them on both sides.
Allow to cool to room temperature and store in a container.

Finishing and presentation

Lay a bed of 20 g of coarse red mojo migas on the dish.
Drain the oil from 4 eggs and coat them with the fine breadcrumb mixture until they are fully covered.
Arrange the 4 eggs on top of the coarse breadcrumbs.
Next to the eggs, sprinkle a smidgen of grey salt so that each diner may season the dish to taste.

Mix the water, salt and vinegar together, and bring to the boil.

1

When the water boils, add the eggs and cook for 1 min 40 sec.

2

COOKING QUAIL EGGS

Quail eggs are a marvellous complement to draw out the utmost flavour from the red mojo coarse breadcrumbs in this recipe. Combined with the cheese, they are reminiscent of the flavour of Almogrote, a cheese-based and slightly spicy pâté typical of the Canarian island of La Gomera.

Drain and cool quickly in iced water.

3

Once cold, peel them carefully, trying not to break them.

4

Rinse with water and dry to remove any remaining shell.

5

Cover them with mild oil and store. They can also be set aside in the red mojo oil described in point 1 on the previous page.

6

CODIUM TEMPURA WITH ITS VINAIGRETTE

X 4

❶ To wash the Codium seaweed
200 g Codium seaweed
500 g mineral water
q.s. ice

❷ For the Codium seaweed juice
100 g Codium seaweed
(the leftovers from the quantity above)
100 g mineral water
q.s. salt
q.s. ice

❸ For the Codium seaweed vinaigrette
100 g Codium seaweed juice
(see point 2)
0.2 g xanthan
5 g lemon juice

❹ For the flour mixture
200 g flour (Las Panaeras)
80 g all-purpose flour
80 g Trisol

❺ For the tempura
80 g strong flour
30 g Trisol
130 g mineral water

❻ For the soy sauce crystals
325 g mineral water
125 g soy sauce
20 g sugar
7 g granulated dashi
7 g xanthan
5 g kombu

❼ For the Japanese mix
5 g red-shiso salt
10 g soy sauce crystals
(see point 6)
5 g granulated dashi
q.s. fine salt
30 g nori seaweed sheets, 20 x 20 cm

Finishing and presentation
200 g olive oil

❶ To wash the Codium seaweed

Wash the seaweed in iced water to remove any grit. Drain and cut into pieces 5 cm long and with at least 3 branches. Divide into four small plastic cups, 25 g per serving, and set aside the least firm and least shiny pieces for point 2.

❷ For the Codium seaweed juice

Bring salted water to the boil (36 g salt per litre of water) and blanch the seaweed for 10 sec. Plunge the seaweed into iced salted water (15 g salt per litre) to cool. Blend the Codium seaweed in an equal quantity of cooling water. Strain the juice obtained through a coarse sieve.

❸ For the Codium seaweed vinaigrette

Put half the Codium seaweed juice in a glass and add the xanthan using a mixer. Remove the air in a vacuum-sealing machine (*or see page 170*) and add the remaining juice. Set aside in the fridge. When serving, add the lemon juice, as it tends to oxidise.

❹ For the flour mixture

Mix all the ingredients and set aside.

❺ For the tempura
Mix the well-chilled water with the remaining ingredients until smooth and set aside in the fridge.

❻ For the soy sauce crystals
See page 95.

❼ For the Japanese mix
Dry the nori seaweed in the oven at 120ºC for 20 min, and then 2 min at 180ºC.
Without letting the nori seaweed cool down, blend all the ingredients to a fine powder in a coffee grinder. Set aside in a bowl.

Finishing and presentation
Dip the Codium seaweed in the flour mix. Heat the oil in a frying pan to 165ºC. Dip the Codium seaweed in the tempura, shake off the excess batter and add each piece, one by one, to the hot oil.
Remove from the oil as it colours, place on a paper towel and dry well without breaking it.
Sprinkle with the Japanese mix.
Dress each portion with 20 g of vinaigrette served in a pipette.

LAS OSTRAS

OYSTER WITH ITS PEARL AND SEA LETTUCE WATER

X 4

1 To prepare the oysters
4 oysters
300 g flake ice
1 kg mineral water
36 g coarse salt

2 For the water smoked with sea lettuce
500 g mineral water
5 g fine salt
0.5 g granulated dashi
5 g sea lettuce

3 For the alginate bath
350 g mineral water
2 g alginate (Algin)

4 For the spherical pearl base
160 g water smoked with sea lettuce *(see point 2)*
25 g mineral water
2 g lemon juice
5 g calcium gluconolactate (Gluco)
1.3 g silver powder
2 g fine salt
0.6 g xanthan

5 For the spherical pearls
q.s. alginate bath *(see point 3)*
q.s. spherical pearl base *(see point 4)*
200 g mineral water
85 g water smoked with sea lettuce *(see point 2)*

6 For the strips of sea lettuce
2 sheets of hydrated sea lettuce *(see point 2)*
20 g water smoked with sea lettuce *(sea point 2)*

Finishing and presentation
q.s. coarse salt
3 pieces of seaweed to decorate

❶ To prepare the oysters
See next page.

❷ For the water smoked with sea lettuce
Mix the water, salt and granulated dashi in a pan and bring to the boil. Remove from the heat and mix with the sea lettuce in a bowl. Cover with plastic wrap. Light a smoking gun with dry vine branches and insert the nozzle under the film for 3 min. Remove the nozzle and smoke for an additional 10 min. Set aside in a bowl.

❸ For the alginate bath
Using a mixer, mix the water and the alginate until fully dissolved.
Let it stand for 2 h in a bowl in the fridge to eliminate the accumulated air bubbles.

❹ For the spherical pearl base
Mix all the liquids together in a mixer, gradually adding the Gluco, silver powder, salt and xanthan.
Remove the air in a vacuum-sealing machine and store in a container in the fridge.
If you do not have a vacuum-sealing machine, *see page 170.*

❺ For the spherical pearls
Fill a semi-spherical 2.5-ml spoon with the spherical pearl base and dip in the alginate bath making pearl-shaped balls (1 pearl per person).
Cook in the alginate bath for 1 min.
Drain from the alginate and rinse with water. Drain again and place in the water smoked with sea lettuce. Store in the fridge.

❻ For the strips of sea lettuce
Spread the sea lettuce out and cut into 16 strips, 1 x 20 mm. Set aside the strips with the water smoked with sea lettuce in an airtight container.

Finishing and presentation
Decorate the dish with a bed of coarse salt and 3 pieces of seaweed. Place the oyster on top without the upper shell.
Dress the oyster with half a spoon of sea lettuce water and arrange 4 strips of sea lettuce around it. Place a pearl on top and the dish may be served.

Prepare 2 baths of iced salt water.

1

Pry the oyster open at the hinge of the shells.

2

HOW TO CLEAN OYSTERS

This procedure is essential for removing any impurities from the oysters. They will therefore appear fresh and glistening in any dish.

Separate the oyster from the adductor muscle.

3

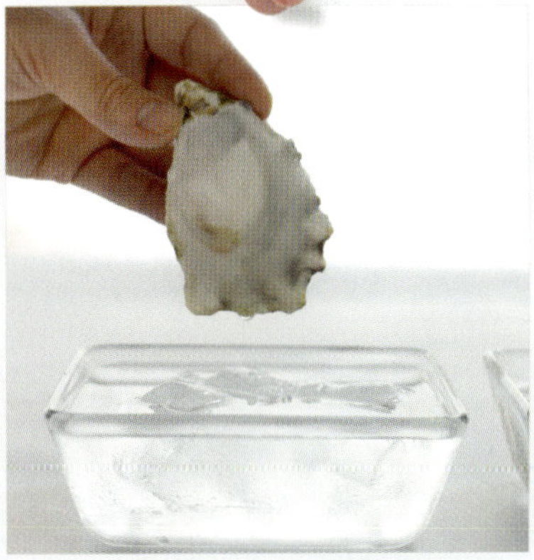

Wash the shell in one of the bowls to remove any impurities.

4

Wash the oyster in the other bowl to remove any impurities and to restore its glossiness.

5

Once the oyster is reassembled, it is ready to serve.

6

OYSTER WITH TARRAGON SHERRY VINEGAR AND VIRGIN OLIVE OIL CAVIAR

X 4

❶ To prepare the oysters
4 oysters
300 g flake ice
1 kg mineral water
36 g coarse salt

❷ For the tarragon sherry vinegar
60 g sherry vinegar
40 g mineral water
10 g fresh tarragon
2 g freshly chopped tarragon
0.1 g xanthan

❸ To drain the oil caviar
q.s. virgin olive oil caviar (Caviaroli)

Finishing and presentation
q.s. coarse salt
3 pieces of seaweed to decorate

❶ To prepare the oysters
See page 49.

❷ For the tarragon sherry vinegar
Mix the vinegar and water in a saucepan and bring to the boil. Remove from the heat, add the unchopped tarragon, cover and set aside so that it infuses for 10 min.
Once the time has elapsed, remove the tarragon and thicken with the xanthan. Remove the air in a vacuum-sealing machine. If you do not have a vacuum-sealing machine, *see page 170*. Before serving the dish, add the chopped tarragon.

❸ To strain the oil caviar
Strain in a sieve and store the caviar in a container.

Finishing and presentation
Decorate the dish with a bed of coarse salt and 3 pieces of seaweed.
Place the oyster on top without the upper shell.
Drizzle a teaspoon of tarragon sherry vinegar over each oyster.
Finish by garnishing the oyster with a small mound of oil caviar.

OYSTER WITH PONZU SAUCE AND SALMON ROE

X 4

1 To prepare the oysters
4 oysters
300 g flake ice
1 kg mineral water
36 g coarse salt

2 To clean the salmon roe
20 g vodka
100 g mineral water
30 g salmon roe

3 For the ponzu sauce
25 g garlic
20 g ginger
350 g mineral water
100 g soy sauce
50 g lemon juice
35 g mirin
5 g granulated dashi

Finishing and presentation
1 lemon
3 pieces of seaweed to decorate
q.s. coarse salt

1 To prepare the oysters

See page 49.

2 To clean the salmon roe

Mix the vodka and water. Dip the roe in the mixture using a slotted spoon and stir in circular motions. Drain and set aside in a container in the fridge.

3 For the ponzu sauce

Crush the unpeeled garlic and thinly slice the ginger.
Mix these two ingredients with all the liquids and the granulated dashi.
Let it stand for 24 h and drain. Set aside in the fridge.

Finishing and presentation

Decorate the dish with a bed of coarse salt and 3 pieces of seaweed.
Cover the oyster with the ponzu sauce and garnish the top with salmon roe.
Grate lemon zest over the oyster and serve.

OYSTER WITH *SUQUET*

X 4

1 To prepare the oysters
4 oysters
300 g flake ice
1 kg mineral water
36 g coarse salt

2 For the marinara sauce
10 g olive oil, 0.4° acidity
5 g garlic
20 g white wine
80 g chopped tomatoes
q.s. paprika
2 bay leaves
q.s. fine salt

3 For the fish stock
250 g fine bones
400 g mineral water
q.s. fine salt

4 For the *suquet* (fish stew)
5 g garlic
25 g olive oil, 0.4° acidity
1 g paprika
125 g marinara sauce *(see point 2)*
125 g peeled and seeded tomatoes
275 g fish stock *(see point 3)*
100 g peeled and roughly chopped Mona Lisa potatoes
q.s. fine salt

Finishing and presentation
q.s. coarse salt
3 pieces of seaweed to decorate
5 g chopped parsley

1 To prepare the oysters
See page 49.

2 For the marinara sauce
Heat the oil in a frying pan on a low heat and sauté the garlic without letting it brown.
Add the white wine and reduce by half.
Add the chopped tomato, paprika and bay leaves, then cook for an additional 15 min.
Add salt as necessary and set aside.

3 For the fish stock
Put the fish bones, water and salt in a saucepan on a low heat. When it begins to boil, leave for 20 min and remove.
Strain through a fine sieve and set aside.

4 For the *suquet* (fish stew)
Put the garlic and oil in a frying pan over the heat and sauté until almost burnt. Remove the garlic and set the oil aside. Allow to cool slightly, add the paprika and fry without letting it burn.
Add the marinara sauce and diced tomato, and allow to cook for 5 min.
Add the fish stock and bring to the boil, then add the potato and cook for 30 min.
Once the potato is cooked, remove it (it will not be used in this recipe).
Add salt as necessary and set aside.

Finishing and presentation
Decorate the dish with a bed of coarse salt and 3 pieces of seaweed.
To heat the oyster, *see page 59*.
Once the oyster is covered with the *suquet* (fish stew), add the chopped parsley. Then serve.

WARM OYSTER IN PICKLING BRINE

X 4

1 To prepare the oysters

4 oysters
300 g flake ice
1 kg mineral water
36 g coarse salt

2 For the pickling brine

15 g garlic
15 g shallot
15 g carrot
120 g olive oil, 0.4° acidity
0.8 g black peppercorns
2 g rosemary
1.5 g thyme
½ bay leaf
5 g salt
30 g white wine
35 g white wine vinegar

Finishing and presentation

3 pieces of seaweed to decorate
q.s. coarse salt

❶ To prepare the oysters

See page 49.

❷ For the pickling brine

Peel and thinly slice the garlic.
Peel and cut the shallot into slices 2 mm thick.
Peel and cut the carrot into slices 1 mm thick.
Put the oil and thinly sliced garlic in a saucepan and heat until the garlic begins to cook.
Then add the shallot, herbs, salt, pepper and carrot.
Add the white wine and cook for 2 min.
Add the vinegar, bring to the boil and remove from the heat.
Store the pickling brine in the fridge.
This pickling brine can be used in many other dishes.

Finishing and presentation

Decorate the dish with a bed of coarse salt and 3 pieces of seaweed.
Warm the oyster as described on the following page.
Decorate with the pickled vegetables arranged on top and serve.

Put the chosen sauce – in this case, the pickling brine – in 2 pans.

1

HOW TO WARM OYSTERS

These simple steps to warm the oysters evenly can be applied to any hot dish in which this bivalve mollusc takes centre stage. Las ostras are high in fat and must be heated in the gentlest possible manner to preserve their texture.

Put the oysters in one of the pans with hot pickling brine that will be used to warm up the oyster and not as a sauce.

2

Warm the oyster shell under the grill.

3

Put the oyster in its shell.

4

Dress the oyster with the pickling brine.

5

OYSTER IN CUCUMBER WATER

X 4

❶ To prepare the oysters
4 oysters
300 g flake ice
1 kg mineral water
36 g coarse salt

❷ For the cucumber water
160 g cucumber
q.s. fine salt
3 g rice vinegar

Finishing and presentation
260 g crushed ice
3 pieces of seaweed to decorate
4 pansy petals
q.s. Tabasco sauce
q.s. extra virgin olive oil

❶ To prepare the oysters

See page 49.

❷ For the cucumber water

Wash and peel the cucumber. Cut it in half and remove the seeds.
Liquidise the cucumber to extract the water. Freeze the cucumber water in a container for 24 h.
Pour the frozen water into a sieve lined with paper towels and let the cucumber water drip through at room temperature: the result will be transparent water.
Add salt as necessary and then the rice vinegar.
Set aside in the fridge.

Finishing and presentation

Decorate the dish with a bed of crushed ice and 3 pieces of seaweed.
Put the oyster in its shell and add 10 g of cucumber water.
Place a pansy petal on the tip of the oyster. On the bottom of the plate, to the side, lay a pipette with Tabasco sauce. Garnish with a drizzle of virgin olive oil and serve.

LAS TAPAS DE LA HUERTA

ANCHOVY AND TOMATO SEEDS ON TOAST

X 4

1 For the toast
¼ coca bread

2 For the textured olive oil
100 g extra virgin olive oil
7 g emulsifier (Glice)
q.s. ice

3 For the silver scales
1 sheet of oblaat
(potato paper), 20 x 10 cm
0.5 g silver powder

4 For the tomato seeds
300 g plum tomatoes

Finishing and presentation
4 anchovy fillets *(see page 67)*
q.s. black peppercorns
q.s. anchovy oil

❶ For the toast

Cut the semi-frozen coca (traditional Mediterranean bread) in slices 5 mm thick.
Place on a tray lined with baking parchment and put pastry weights on top. First bake for 20 min at 120ºC, then for 5 min at 160ºC.
Allow to cool to room temperature and store in a container.

❷ For the textured olive oil

Dissolve the emulsifier with half the oil in a pan at 50ºC.
Once dissolved, add the other half of the oil at room temperature and mix.
Stir the mixture steadily with a spatula in a bain marie with ice until it thickens and takes on a butter-like consistency.
Store in a container in the fridge. The bread will not moisten as fast thanks to this oil.

❸ For the silver scales

Manipulate the oblaat with your hands, forming a ball.
Using scissors, cut it into irregular-shaped strips 5 x 2 mm.
Place in a container and add the silver powder.
Cover the container and shake well so that the silver powder adheres to the oblaat. Go over any pieces that are too large with the scissors.
Allow to cool to room temperature in a dry place.

❹ For the tomato seeds

Using a knife, cut the two ends of the tomato until the inside seeds are visible.
Cut the tomato without breaking the placenta (the part of the tomato containing the seeds). Using the knife, remove the entire placenta (two per person are needed) and store in a container in the fridge.
Keep the rest of the tomato for other dishes.

Finishing and presentation

Spread the thinnest layer of textured oil on the toast.
On top of the oil, place two tomato seeds, followed by an anchovy, with the skin facing upwards. Dress lightly with a drizzle of anchovy oil and freshly ground black pepper.
Arrange 4 or 5 silver scales on top of the anchovy and serve.

Soak the anchovies in water for a minimum of 15 min.

1

Using scissors, cut the tail and slit open the stomach.

2

CLEANING SALTED ANCHOVIES

To clean salted anchovies, you just have to follow these steps. However, the end result is not always the same. It must be borne in mind that anchovies are cured, desalinated and pressed differently in every jar.

Remove the bone.

3

Using tweezers, remove all the bones from the stomach.

4

Allow the anchovies to dry.

5

Cover with oil.

6

ROASTED LEEK WITH ASH-INFUSED VINAIGRETTE

X 4

1 For the roasted leek in almond oil

4 leeks
20 g sunflower oil
20 g almond oil
q.s. fine salt
q.s. black pepper

2 For the ash-infused vinaigrette

60 g oil blend *(see point 1)*
6 g charred leek skin *(see point 1)*
6 g white wine vinegar
q.s. fine salt

Finishing and presentation

6 whole raw almonds
q.s. fine salt
q.s. black pepper

1 For the roasted leek in almond oil

Wash and slice off the end of the leek's green leaves, leaving just the white stalk.
Roast in the oven (a charcoal oven is best) at 180°C until well roasted and fully charred on the outside. Once ready, wrap the leek in aluminium foil and let it stand for a few hours.
Remove the outer part of the leek and set aside the charred skin.
Season the leeks with salt and pepper and store them in a vacuum bag with the oil blend.
Remove 80% of the air in a vacuum-sealing machine. Set aside.
If you do not have a vacuum-sealing machine, *see page 170*.

2 For the ash-infused vinaigrette

Open the vacuum bag, drain the leeks and use the oil blend for this dish. Choose the most charred leek skin and dehydrate in a dehydrator or oven at 50°C for 12 h. Then grind the leek to a fine powder in a coffee grinder.
Emulsify the oil blend with the vinegar, salt and ash using a whisk.
Set aside in the fridge.

Finishing and presentation

Cut the leeks into 4-cm pieces and season with salt and pepper.
Arrange 6 pieces of leek on an elongated dish, dress with the ash-infused vinaigrette and grate the almond over the leek just before serving.

ARTICHOKES WITH IDIAZÁBAL CHEESE CREAM AND MOROCCAN LEMON

X 4

1 For the artichoke confit
8 artichokes
1 kg mineral water
80 g olive oil, 0.4° acidity
4 g lemon juice
2 g salt

2 For the Idiazábal cheese cream
60 g smoked Idiazábal cheese
60 g milk
60 g cream, 35% fat
1 g salt

3 For the pickled Moroccan lemon
1 lemon
100 g coarse salt
25 g lemon juice

Finishing and presentation
q.s. black pepper
q.s. extra virgin olive oil
q.s. shavings of Idiazábal cheese

❶ For the artichoke confit

See next page.

❷ For the Idiazábal cheese cream

Grate the cheese very finely.
In a saucepan, mix the milk, cream and grated cheese and melt on a low heat. Add salt as necessary and strain through a fine sieve. Set aside in the fridge.

❸ For the pickled Moroccan lemon

Place the whole lemon in a container, cover with salt and pour over the lemon juice. Let it stand in the fridge for 1 month. Given the lengthy process, preparing more than one lemon is recommended.
Once this time has elapsed, remove from the fridge, wash and peel the lemon without the pith. Cut the lemon peel into 2 mm-cubes. Set aside in the fridge.

Finishing and presentation

Heat the Idiazábal cream in a saucepan on a low heat.
In a semi-shallow round dish, add 30 g of Idiazábal cream. Spread the artichokes unevenly on the dish. Season with pepper and diced pickled lemon.
Finally, top each artichoke with a shaving of cheese, drizzle with virgin olive oil and serve.

Mix the water and the lemon juice in a bowl and set aside.

1

Clean the artichokes, cut off the stalk, outer leaves and the top, leaving just the heart.

2

HOW TO PREPARE ARTICHOKES

Artichoke hearts are used in many recipes. However, cutting this vegetable, without it turning brown when exposed to the air, and then cooking it is an arduous task for many. Follow these steps to make its preparation easier and savour delicious artichokes al dente. If you do not have a vacuum-sealing machine, *see page 170*.

Cut the hearts into quarters and set aside in the fridge in lemon and water.

3

Bring a pan of water and salt to the boil. When boiling, add the artichokes and cook from 6 to 8 min, until al dente. Cooking time depends on their size and the season.

4

Take the artichokes off the heat and plunge into a bath of iced water and salt to cool. Then dry.

5

Place 80 g portions of artichokes with 20 g olive oil in vacuum bags. Remove 85% of the air in a vacuum-sealing machine. Set aside.

6

ARTICHOKES WITH CURED HAM AND PARSLEY GELATIN

X 4

1 For the ham stock
100 g ham trimmings
200 g mineral water

2 For the thickened ham stock
200 g ham stock *(see point 1)*
0.6 g xanthan

3 For the boiled artichokes
800 g artichokes
(250 g will remain)
400 g mineral water
5 g salt

4 For the infused artichokes
250 g boiled artichokes
40 g olive oil, 0.4° acidity

5 For the crackling pork cubes
20 g ham fat
50 g sunflower oil

6 For the parsley gelatin
100 g parsley leaves
100 g mineral water
q.s. salt
1 gelatin sheet
1 g agar

7 For the strands of black garlic
1 g black garlic

Finishing and presentation
q.s. extra virgin olive oil
q.s. black pepper

1 For the ham stock

Cut the ham into 3 cm cubes and simmer very gently in a pan with water for 40 min.
Remove from the heat and allow to infuse for an additional 20 min.
Strain through a fine sieve and then paper towels. Set aside in the fridge.

2 For the thickened ham stock

Mix 100 g ham stock with the xanthan in a mixer until well dissolved. Remove the air in a vacuum-sealing machine and add the remaining juice. If you do not have a vacuum-sealing machine, *see page 170*.
Set aside until use.

3 For the boiled artichokes

See up to point 5 on page 73.

4 For the infused artichokes

Pack 7 or 8 pieces (between 60 and 65 g) of boiled artichokes in vacuum bags with a little olive oil and remove the air in a vacuum-sealing machine. Set aside the portions in the fridge.
If you do not have a vacuum-sealing machine, *see page 170*.

5 For the crackling pork cubes

Cut the ham fat into 0.5 x 0.5 cm cubes.
Fry them in a pan on a low heat with sunflower oil until golden and crisp. Set aside on paper towels.

6 For the parsley gelatin

Blanch the parsley leaves in a pan with boiling water for 5 sec. Then plunge into iced water to cool.
Drain, add salt, blend in the water with a mixer and strain through a fine sieve.
Bring one third of the parsley water to the boil, thicken with the agar and the gelatin sheet, and add the remaining parsley water.
Mix well and pour the mixture into a bowl at least 3 cm in height. Leave to set in the fridge for 2 h.
Then cut into 5 x 5-mm cubes.

7 For the strands of black garlic

Peel the garlic and cut into strands 2 x 10 mm.
Set aside in a bowl in the fridge.

Finishing and presentation
Put the bag with the artichokes in a bain marie at 65°C for 4 min. Heat the thickened ham stock until it comes to the boil. On each warmed dish, arrange the artichokes unevenly and dress with 20 g thickened ham stock. Place 6 cubes of gelatin between the artichokes. Put one crackling pork cube on top of each artichoke and, next to the artichokes, a strand of black garlic. Warm under the grill. Just before serving, sprinkle with freshly ground pepper and drizzle with extra virgin olive oil.

AVOCADO MASH WITH SEA URCHINS, SEAWEED AND PARSLEY CHLOROPHYLL

X 4

1 For the sea urchin roe
1.5 kg sea urchins
(150 g clean sea urchin roe)
20 g mineral water
q.s. fine salt

2 For the sea urchin sauce
50 g broken or less aesthetic sea urchin roe *(see point 1)*

3 For the Codium seaweed water
100 g fresh Codium seaweed
100 g mineral water
q.s. salt

4 For the parsley water
80 g fresh parsley, stalks removed
q.s. mineral water
q.s. salt

5 For the Codium seaweed and parsley chlorophyll
80 g parsley water *(see point 4)*
80 g Codium seaweed water *(see point 3)*
0.3 g xanthan

Finishing and presentation
2 avocados (300 g each)
q.s. fine salt
q.s. black peppercorns
2 fresh lemons
40 g extra virgin olive oil

1 For the sea urchin roe
Mix the water and salt, and set aside. To open the sea urchins, cut at the base using scissors, making a circle 2 cm in diameter. Remove the roe from the sea urchins and rinse in a bath of water and salt to remove any impurities.
Dry on paper towels, separating the whole roe from the broken roe.
Divide the whole roe into 20 g-portions and set the broken roe aside to prepare the sauce. Set aside in the fridge.

2 For the sea urchin sauce
Strain the broken sea urchin roe through a sieve using a spoon to obtain a thin sauce.
Pour into a bottle and store in the fridge.

3 For the Codium seaweed water
Bring salted water to the boil (36 g salt per litre of water) and blanch the seaweed for 10 sec. Plunge into salted iced water (15 g salt per litre) to cool.
Blend the Codium seaweed in an equal quantity of cooling water. Strain the juice obtained through a fine sieve (100 g of codium juice will be obtained).

4 For the parsley water
Blanch the parsley in boiling salted water (18 g salt per litre). Plunge into salted cold water (18 g salt per litre) to cool.
Blend the parsley in an equal quantity of cooling water. Strain the juice obtained through a fine sieve (80 g of parsley water will be obtained).

5 For the Codium seaweed and parsley chlorophyll
In a bowl, mix half the parsley water with half the Codium seaweed water.
Dissolve the xanthan in the above mixture and blend in a mixer until a smooth sauce is obtained. Remove the air in a vacuum-sealing machine (or *see page 170*), add the remaining waters and mix.
Set aside in the fridge.

Finishing and presentation
Using a knife, cut through the centre of the avocado lengthwise until the knife comes in contact with the pit. Separate the two halves, set aside one of them for another portion and make cuts in the avocado flesh from right to left.
Scoop out the avocado flesh with a spoon and put in a bowl. Dress each dish with salt, pepper, the juice of half a lemon and extra virgin olive oil. Mash with a spoon until a guacamole-like texture is obtained.
Place the avocado in the centre of the dish and top with the sea urchin roe (20 g). Add 8 g of sea urchin sauce and drizzle the well-chilled seaweed and parsley chlorophyll around the avocado. Repeat the procedure three times.

TOMATO TARTARE

X 4

❶ For the tomato cubes
350 g tomatoes

❷ For the tomato tartare
200 g tomato cubes
(see point 1)
25 g tomato nectar (Travol)
12 g Dijon mustard
8 g Worcestershire sauce (Perrins)
3 g HP sauce
3 g fine salt
3 g chopped basil
0.7 g habanero chilli pepper sauce
0.3 g dried oregano

❸ For the slices of bread
20 slices of bread (Gutiattu)

Finishing and presentation
12 sprouts (Sakura Mix)
4 basil leaves
5 g capers
q.s. black pepper
15 g extra virgin olive oil

❶ For the tomato cubes
Peel and slice the tomatoes.
Drain and discard the juice.
Chop the flesh into 2-mm cubes, without letting it become a purée, and let it stand over a colander to drain off the excess water.
Some 200 g drained tomato cubes will be obtained.

❷ For the tomato tartare
Mix all the ingredients, except the tomato, together.
Add the tomato to this mixture, stir gently without breaking the cubes and allow to drain in a colander for 1 h.
Add salt as necessary and then set aside, covered, in the fridge.

❸ For the slices of bread
Spread the slices of bread between two oven racks. Bake at 150ºC for 6 min until golden on both sides.
Allow to cool and store in a container.

Finishing and presentation
Choose 5 bunches of each sprout.
Choose the basil leaves.
Drain and set the capers aside.
Arrange 50 g tomato tartare in the centre of a dish and spread into a circle with a diameter of 16 cm. Grind two turns of the pepper mill over the tartare.
Drizzle a splash of olive oil around the tartare.
Put 3 capers around the tartare, and top with 2 purple sprouts and 2 green sprouts.
Chop the basil leaves into thin strips and spread evenly over the tartare. Serve.

Natalia Fara

Lorena Cuello
TICKETS
Bilal el Meghoui

Xavi Alba
Rachid Kollech
Laia Caner
Guille Miret

J. Miguel Estrada

THE ORIGIN
TICKETS
Fran Agudo
Jon Urruti
Rubén González

ARTICHOKE HEART WITH QUAIL EGG YOLK AND SALMON ROE

X 4

❶ For the artichoke hearts
4 artichokes
1 kg mineral water
3 g ascorbic acid

❷ To the artichokes confit
4 artichoke hearts *(see point 1)*
500 g olive oil, 0.4° acidity

❸ For the quail egg yolks
4 quail eggs
50 g sunflower oil

❹ To clean the salmon roe
25 g salmon roe
25 g vodka (or sake)
50 g mineral water

Finishing and presentation
q.s. Maldon salt
q.s. fine salt

❶ For the artichoke hearts

Mix the ascorbic acid and water. Remove the outer greener leaves of the artichoke to reach the paler green inner leaves. Trim the stem and chop 5 cm off the top of the artichoke, leaving just the heart.
Turn the artichoke until it is 4 cm in diameter and 2 cm in height, without leaving any thorns and it is fully rounded. Using a scooper, make a hole in the centre of the heart 2 cm wide and 1 cm deep. Set aside the hearts in the water with the ascorbic acid.

❷ To the artichokes confit

Put the turned artichokes in the oil in a pan on a low heat.
Cook at 100°C for 35 min until fully tender.
Remove from the heat and allow to cool.

❸ For the quail egg yolks

Using a knife, make a cut in the narrowest part of the egg, 5 mm below the tip.
Finish breaking the shell and separate the yolk from the white. Discard the white and put the yolk in a container, fully covered by the sunflower oil to prevent it from drying out. Set aside in the fridge.

❹ To clean the salmon roe

Mix the vodka and water. Dip the roe in the mixture using a slotted spoon and stir in a circular motion.
Remove and drain, placing paper towels beneath the spoon, and store in a container. Set aside in the fridge.

Finishing and presentation

Drain the artichokes from the oil and add fine salt as necessary.
Remove the egg yolks with a slotted spoon, drain off the excess oil and place them in the artichoke heart.
Put the artichokes in the oven at 70°C to keep them warm.
Sprinkle salt over the yolk and warm under the grill for 5 sec.
An idea for presenting the dish: cover it with clean and dry straw and a 9 x 9 cm crumpled piece of baking parchment.
Serve one artichoke per portion and top with 4 g of salmon roe and half the yolk. Sprinkle Maldon salt over the roe. Finally, cover with a hood, smoke with a smoking gun for 5 sec and serve.

WHITE ASPARAGUS SPEARS WITH PARMESAN CREAM

X 4

❶ For the white asparagus spears
12 white asparagus spears
3 g ascorbic acid
3 kg mineral water
35 g fine salt

❷ For the parmesan cheese cream
120 g parmesan cheese
200 g full-fat milk
1 g fine salt
0.5 g freshly ground pepper
0.6 g xanthan

Finishing and presentation
50 g parmesan cheese
10 g black olive paste (Marchenica)
1 orange
50 g extra virgin olive oil

❶ For the white asparagus spears

Mix the ascorbic acid with 1 kg of water.
Cut the asparagus into 15-cm pieces.
Lightly peel the asparagus and place in the water and ascorbic acid mixture to prevent oxidation.
Boil the rest of the water with the salt.
Cook the asparagus for 8 min (depending on the thickness).
Once cooked, drain carefully to prevent breaking and allow to cool with the cooking liquid to room temperature. Leave in the cooking liquid in the fridge.

❷ For the parmesan cheese cream

Remove the cheese rind and cut into pieces.
Put the milk and the cheese in the food processor at 70ºC and speed 7 for 2 min, and add salt and pepper as necessary. Strain through a fine sieve.
Blend half the liquid with the xanthan in a mixer until well dissolved.
Add the rest of the mixture and set aside in the fridge.

Finishing and presentation

Warm up the asparagus to room temperature 1 h before serving.
To prepare each dish, dry 3 asparagus spears on paper towels and cut them in half.
Put a line of parmesan cheese cream (30 g) on the bottom of the dish.
Place the asparagus on top of the cream, alternating the two halves.
Grate the parmesan cheese over the asparagus.
On one end of the asparagus put a dab of black olive paste, and on the other, a dab of orange zest.
Finish by drizzling olive oil over the asparagus.

TOMATO SALAD WITH TRANSPARENT GAZPACHO GELATIN

X 4

❶ For the transparent gazpacho water
60 g spring onion
1 kg plum tomatoes
60 g cucumber
50 g green pepper
q.s. fine salt

❷ For the transparent gazpacho gelatin
500 g transparent gazpacho water *(see point 1)*
3 gelatin sheets

❸ For the thick herb vinaigrette
70 g olive oil, 0.4° acidity
6 g white wine vinegar
4 g fresh mint
3 g fresh parsley
2 g coriander berries
1 g lemon thyme
q.s. fine salt

❹ For the peeled cherry tomatoes
36 seasonal cherry tomatoes (our favourite is the Ugly Tudela variety)
q.s. mineral water
q.s. ice

Finishing and presentation
36 basil sprouts
q.s. extra virgin olive oil
q.s. salt
q.s. ground black pepper

❶ For the transparent gazpacho water

Cut the spring onion into quarters and blanch three times in water. Put all the ingredients together in a mixer and blend at speed 8 for 3 min.
Store the gazpacho purée in a container in the freezer for 24 h. Once this time has elapsed, remove from the freezer and allow to thaw for 20 min so that it may be broken into pieces.
Pour into a sieve lined with paper towels and let the gazpacho water drain for 5 h: the result will be transparent water.

❷ For the transparent gazpacho gelatin

Soak the gelatin in the gazpacho water and let it hydrate for 1 h. Drain the gelatin sheets. Heat some gazpacho water in a pan and dissolve the gelatin. Once dissolved, mix with the remaining gazpacho water.
Leave to set in a container in the fridge.

❸ For the thick herb vinaigrette

Put all the ingredients into a mixing glass and blend in a mixer to a fine consistency.

❹ For the peeled cherry tomatoes

Make a small incision in each tomato.
Put water in a pan to boil, blanch the tomatoes for a few seconds and plunge into iced water to cool.
Drain and peel the tomatoes.
Set aside in a bowl in the fridge.

Finishing and presentation

Lay a bed of 50 g of gazpacho water gelatin on a dish.
Serve 8 tomatoes per portion, interspersing them with the gelatin, and season with salt and pepper.
Garnish each piece of tomato with a basil leaf. Dress each tomato with a splash of olive oil and a drizzle of the thick herb vinaigrette.

ORANGE SALAD WITH OLIVE JUICE NECTAR

X 4

❶ For the olive juice
250 g Gordal olive juice
0.6 g xanthan

❷ For the orange segments and julienned peel
4 oranges

❸ For the syrup
100 g sugar
100 g mineral water

❹ For the julienned lemon peel
1 lemon
40 g syrup in equal quantities *(see point 3)*

❺ For the chilli oil
10 g olive oil, 0.4° acidity
1 dry chilli
q.s. fine salt

Finishing and presentation
q.s. ground cumin
q.s. ras el hanout
q.s. fine salt
q.s. black pepper
36 mint leaves
4 g sprigs mint
20 g virgin olive oil

❶ For the olive juice

See page 17.
Add the xanthan to the olive juice and blend in a mixer to a creamy and smooth sauce. Pour into a bottle and store in the fridge.

❷ For the orange segments and julienned peel

Peel 1 orange with a vegetable peeler (avoiding the pith) and cut the peel into long julienne strips. Store chilled covered with damp paper towels.
Peel the rest of the oranges without the pith, as well as the segments. Store the orange segments, well-covered, in the fridge.

❸ For the syrup

Mix the two ingredients and bring to the boil until the sugar dissolves. Remove from the heat and allow to cool.

❹ For the julienned lemon peel

Clean and peel the lemon with a vegetable peeler (avoiding the pith) and cut into long julienne strips.
Put the peel in the syrup and set aside.

❺ For the chilli oil

Put the oil with the crushed chilli and the salt in a pan on a low heat.
Sauté for 10 min and remove from the heat.
Pour into a bottle and set aside.

Finishing and presentation

Pour 20 g of olive juice into the bottom of a bowl. Arrange 9 orange segments in a fan shape. Season the orange with the cumin, the ras el hanout, the salt and the freshly ground black pepper. Garnish with 5 strips of orange peel and 5 strips of lemon peel on top.
Put a drop of chilli oil between each segment.
On top of each segment, place a mint leaf, and in the centre, a sprig of mint.
Finish by drizzling a splash of olive oil around the orange segments and serve.

LAS TAPITAS DEL MAR

RAZOR CLAMS IN PICKLING BRINE WITH SAFFRON PEARLS AND SOY SAUCE CRYSTALS

X 4

❶ **To cook the razor clams**
800 g razor clams (50 g/unit)
1 kg mineral water
30 g salt
q.s. ice

❷ **For the soy sauce crystals**
250 g mineral water
100 g soy sauce
15 g sugar
5 g granulated dashi
5 g kombu
5 g xanthan

❸ **For the white wine pickling sauce**
50 g garlic
300 g olive oil, 0.4° acidity
75 g white wine
50 g sherry vinegar
1 bay leaf
1 sprig thyme
1 sprig rosemary
50 g carrot
50 g shallot
q.s. xanthan
125 g mineral water
5 g fine salt
20 g black peppercorns

❹ **For the saffron water**
100 g mineral water
0.3 g saffron
q.s. fine salt

❺ **For the saffron pearls**
100 g mineral water
2 g fine salt
20 g tapioca pearls
16 g saffron water
(see point 4)

❻ **For the pickled red onion**
25 g red onion
25 g pickling brine
(see point 3)

❼ **For the julienned tarragon**
16 tarragon leaves
q.s. mineral water
q.s. ice

Finishing and presentation
16 Sakura Mix sprouts

❶ To cook the razor clams

Put the razor clams in a bowl that allows them to remain firm and upright.
Fill the bowl with salted cold water and purge the razor clams for 1 h.
Once purged, sort by size and put about 14 of them in each vacuum bag.
Remove 95% of the air in a vacuum-sealing machine.
Cook the razor clams inside the bag in boiling water for 50 sec (the cooking time may vary according to the size). Plunge the razor clams into iced water to cool.
Open the bags, take out the razor clams and remove them from the shell, keeping the most aesthetic shellfish. If you do not have a vacuum bag, *see page 170*.
Remove the stomach and mouth of the razor clams without distorting the original shape; cut them in half, reassemble the razor clams in the shell that was set aside.
Each diner will be given a 200 g serving (between 3 and 6 units, depending on the weight).

❷ For the soy sauce crystals

See next page.

❸ For the white wine pickling sauce

Crush the unpeeled garlic and sauté in the oil on a low heat.
Put the white wine in a saucepan and reduce by half. Then add the water, vinegar, herbs, the julienned carrot and the sliced shallot and cook for 10 min.
Add the garlic oil, add salt and black pepper as necessary and cook for 5 min.
Allow the sauce to macerate for 3 h.
Decant the pickling brine and thicken the liquid part with xanthan in a ratio of 0.4 g per litre of liquid. Then gradually mix with the fat part using a blender. Store in a squeeze bottle in the fridge.

❹ For the saffron water

Boil the water with the salt and, once removed from the heat, add the saffron. Leave to infuse for 3 h.

❺ For the saffron pearls

Mix the water and salt, bring to the boil, add the tapioca, cook for 16 min and let it stand for an additional 5 min.
Drain in a colander and mix with the saffron water. Set aside and leave to infuse for 6 h.

❻ For the pickled red onion

Peel the onion and remove the first three layers. Cut in half and into julienne strips 4 cm long x 1 cm wide. Add to the pickling brine, cook on a low heat for 5 min and set aside.

❼ For the julienned tarragon

Cut each tarragon leaf in two and set aside in iced water.

Finishing and presentation

Arrange the razor clams on a dish and cover with the pickling brine. Put a piece of red onion on the two ends of the razor clam, and alongside, 5 saffron pearls.
Top the pearls with a piece of julienned tarragon and a Sakura sprout.
Just before serving, place a piece of soy sauce crystal next to each sprout.

Heat the water and add the sugar, kombu and granulated dashi.

1

Remove from the heat and add the soy. Leave to infuse for 24 h in the fridge.

2

SOY SAUCE CRYSTALS

The soy sauce crystal technique proves very interesting in cooking. The texture of savoury caramel is obtained, a characteristic feature of these razor clams in pickling brine with saffron pearls. If you do not have a vacuum-sealing machine to prepare this dish, *see page 170.*

Once it has stood, blend the soy base with the xanthan.

3

Put the mixture in a vacuum bag, remove the air in a vacuum-sealing machine and set aside. With a palette knife, spread to a thickness of 1 mm in the dehydrator.

4

Allow to dry in a dehydrator or oven at 45°C for 24 h.

5

Once dry, break the crystals, into 5 mm pieces approx., and store in a container with packets of silica gel.

6

RAZOR CLAMS WITH *REFRITO* SAUCE AND LEMON AIR

X 4

1 To cook the razor clams
800 g razor clams (50 g/unit)
1 kg mineral water
30 g salt
q.s. ice

2 For the garlic oil
90 g garlic
(80 g finely sliced garlic)
100 g olive oil, 0.4° acidity

3 For the *refrito* sauce
500 g mineral water
6 g granulated dashi
25 g soy sauce
2 g xanthan
30 g white wine vinegar
80 g garlic oil *(see point 2)*
1 g fine salt

4 For the lemon air
200 g lemon juice
300 g mineral water
6 g Sucro emulsifier

Finishing and presentation
1 kg coarse salt
q.s. chive blossoms

1 To cook the razor clams
See point 1 on page 94.

2 For the garlic oil
Peel and finely slice the garlic with a mandolin.
Heat the oil on a low heat and sauté the finely sliced garlic without allowing it to brown.
Remove from the heat and set aside.

3 For the *refrito* sauce
Boil the water, granulated dashi and soy sauce, and thicken with the xanthan.
Mix the vinegar with the garlic oil and add to the previous mixture.
Bring to the boil and add salt as necessary. Drain and allow to cool.

4 For the lemon air
Mix the water and the lemon juice in a bowl. Add the Sucro to the previous mixture and stir.
The air is prepared just before serving the dish.

Finishing and presentation
Using a blender, whisk the lemon air mixture until it increases in volume; let it stand for 30 sec.
Arrange the razor clams on a dish with coarse salt and cover each one with the *refrito* sauce.
Add a dollop of lemon air to the other end, using two spoons.
Finish by garnishing the lemon air with a chive blossom.

LETTUCE TACO WITH CEVICHE

X 4

1 To clean the corvina
250 g corvina fillet

2 For the *leche de tigre* (Peruvian marinade)
6 g garlic
0.5 g red chilli
350 g lime juice
80 g white fish
15 g celery
5 g ginger
20 g white onion
3 g fresh coriander
300 g sparkling mineral water
2 g fine salt
1.4 g xanthan

3 For the iceberg lettuce taco
4 iceberg lettuces

4 For the fried garlic
10 g garlic
100 g olive oil, 0.4° acidity

5 For the nori seaweed
50 g nori seaweed strips

6 For the kimchi sauce crystal
100 g kimchi sauce
0.6 g xanthan

7 For the celery sticks
50 g celery stalk

8 For the apple brunoise
0.3 g ascorbic acid
100 g mineral water
70 g Granny Smith apple

9 For the julienned lime
1 lime

Finishing and presentation
q.s. salt
q.s. black pepper
25 mg extra virgin olive oil
4 coriander sprouts

1 To clean the corvina

Remove the scales and skin, wash and fillet the corvina, trying to leave the fillet as whole as possible. Cut the fillet in half lengthwise, dividing it in two and removing the central bone. Cut into fingers 3.5 cm long x 3 mm thick. Set aside in the fridge.

2 For the *leche de tigre*

Using a mixer or food processor, blend the garlic, chilli, lime juice, white fish, celery, peeled ginger, onion and coriander stalks.
Add the sparkling water, strain through a fine sieve and add salt as necessary.
Finally, bind with the xanthan.

3 For the iceberg lettuce taco

Cut the lettuce stalk and separate the lettuce leaf by leaf without breaking them, discarding the first soft leaves.
Choose the most flexible leaves and cut slices of lettuce with a round pastry cutter 8 cm in diameter. Layer the slices of lettuce in a container between damp paper towels to prevent them from drying out. Store in the fridge.

4 For the fried garlic

Peel the garlic. Thinly slice the garlic with a mandolin. Put the oil in a pan with the garlic on a low heat, and when it begins to turn golden, remove, drain and dry on a paper towel. Set aside.

❺ For the nori seaweed
Cut the seaweed into julienne strips 1 mm x 3 cm long , and set aside in a container with a packet of silica gel.

❻ For the kimchi sauce crystal
Using a mixer, emulsify the kimchi sauce with the xanthan. Spread the mixture over a silicone tray to a thickness of 1 mm and dry in a dehydrator or oven at 50°C for 12 h. Remove the dehydrated kimchi and store in a container with a packet of silica gel.

❼ For the celery sticks
Thinly slice the celery to a thickness of 3 mm with a mandolin, discarding the green part and leaving just the paler part. Cut into julienne strips 3 cm long x 3 mm thick, and set aside wrapped in a damp paper towel in the fridge.

❽ For the apple brunoise
Dissolve the ascorbic acid in the water. Peel the apple with a vegetable peeler and thinly slice to a thickness of 3 mm with a mandolin. Cut into 3-mm julienne strips and then dice into 3-mm cubes. Set the apple aside in the prepared water.

❾ For the julienned lime
Cut the lime peel into julienne strips 1 cm long x 1 mm wide. Set aside wrapped in a damp paper towel in the fridge.

Finishing and presentation
To prepare each wedge: freshly marinade 15 g of corvina in the *leche de tigre* and season with salt and pepper. Lay the marinated corvina in the centre of the lettuce.
On the fish part, place 6 apple cubes; on the top part, a strip of lime peel; in the central part, a celery stick, laid diagonally; and in the centre, a slice of garlic and 1 coriander sprout.
Break the kimchi crystal by hand and sprinkle on top. Dress with virgin olive oil and, finally, add the julienned nori to afford volume.

FISH COATED WITH RED MOJO

X 4

1 To clean the corvina
700 g corvina

2 For the red mojo sauce
150 g Canarian red pepper (or choricero pepper paste)
100 g white wine vinegar
20 g garlic
8 g freshly chopped parsley
8 g dried oregano
6 g dried cumin
5 g paprika
4 g black peppercorns
q.s. fine salt
40 g mineral water

3 For the red mojo mayonnaise
40 g mayonnaise
40 g red mojo sauce
(see point 2)

4 For the flour mixture
200 g flour (Las Panaeras)
80 g all-purpose flour
80 g soluble wheat-derived fibre (Trisol)

Finishing and presentation
920 g olive oil, 0.4° acidity
q.s. salt

1 To clean the corvina

Remove the scales and fillet the corvina, trying to leave the fillet as whole as possible when removing the skin. Divide the fillet lengthwise into 2 parts. Remove the central bone and any dark parts. Cut into pieces 5 cm long by 3 cm wide.
Set aside in the fridge.

2 For the red mojo sauce

Blend all the ingredients except the water in a mixer, and set aside 40 g of this mixture to prepare the mayonnaise.
Add the water and mix.
Pass through a sieve and set aside in the fridge.

3 For the red mojo mayonnaise

Mix the two ingredients together with a whisk and store in a bottle in the fridge.

4 For the flour mixture

Mix the three ingredients together and set aside.

Finishing and presentation

Freshly marinade 100 g of corvina in the sauce.
Drain, dip in the flour mixture and then place in the sieve to remove the excess.
Put the fish in the deep-fat fryer with olive oil at 200ºC and leave for 1 min 15 sec until golden.
Dry on paper towels, season with salt on both sides, put 3 dabs of mojo mayonnaise on each piece of fish and serve.

BABY CUTTLEFISH WITH INK VINAIGRETTE AND MENTAIKO

X 4

1 To clean the baby cuttlefish
400 g fresh baby cuttlefish

2 For the baby squid base
15 g olive oil, 0.4° acidity
1 clove of garlic
60 g onion
140 g baby squid
q.s. fine salt
60 g white wine
250 g mineral water

3 For the soy sauce crystals
250 g mineral water
5 g granulated dashi
15 g sugar
100 g soy sauce
5 g kombu
5 g xanthan

4 For the squid vinaigrette
40 g baby squid base
(see point 2)
40 g squid ink
10 g white wine vinegar
15 g olive oil, 0.4° acidity
q.s. chopped chives

5 For the mentaiko vinaigrette
60 g mentaiko
20 g mineral water
20 g olive oil, 0.4° acidity
q.s. fine salt

Finishing and presentation
q.s. toasted white sesame

1 To clean the baby cuttlefish

Remove the cuttlebone carefully so as not to break the intestinal sac.
Using scissors, remove the mouth and the eyes and set aside.
Rinse with water to remove any possible grit and dry on paper towels.
Cut out pieces of baking parchment measuring 8 x 5 cm to wrap 80-g portions of cuttlefish.
Store in the fridge.

2 For the baby squid base

Sauté the minced garlic clove and chopped onion in the oil. Add the sliced baby squid, season with salt and sauté.
Drizzle with white wine, allow to reduce and add the water.
Cook on a low heat for 30 min until a thick and flavoursome base is obtained.
Strain through a fine sieve and store in the fridge.

3 For the soy sauce crystals

See page 95.

4 For the squid vinaigrette

In a saucepan, mix the baby squid base with the squid ink and the white wine vinegar.
Bring to a boil, remove from the heat, add the oil to cut the vinegar and, finally, add the chopped chives.

5 For the mentaiko vinaigrette

Mix all the ingredients together and set aside.

Finishing and presentation

Add salt to the baby cuttlefish as necessary and roast in a non-stick saucepan on both sides, until golden and juicy.
Arrange on a dish and drizzle lightly with some ink vinaigrette and a few drops of mentaiko over the tentacles.
Sprinkle some white toasted sesame and crushed soy sauce crystals over the baby cuttlefish.
Serve.

SQUID IN ITS INK

X 4

1 To clean the squid
700 g squid (30-35 g/unit)

2 For the fish stock
700 g fish bones
1 kg mineral water
15 g fine salt

3 For the *sofrito* (sautéd garlic, onion and tomato base)
15 g garlic
50 g olive oil, 0.4° acidity
400 g onion
1 sprig thyme
1 sprig rosemary
2 bay leaves
80 g fresh tomato
20 g chopped tomatoes
q.s. fine salt

4 To blanch the veal cheek
200 g veal cheek
1 kg mineral water
15 g white wine vinegar
10 g fine salt

5 For the squid stuffing
150 g squid tentacles and fins *(see point 1)*
70 g sofrito *(see point 3)*
200 g chopped veal cheek mixture *(see point 4)*
2 g paprika
50 g fish stock *(see point 2)*
50 g mineral water
5 g Iberian ham fat
q.s. salt and pepper

6 For the squid base
3 g garlic
110 g onion
25 g olive oil, 0.4° acidity
200 g squid cuts
130 g white wine
1 kg mineral water
q.s. fine salt

7 To stuff the squid
12 clean squid tubes
180 g stuffing *(see point 5)*

8 For the squid stew
16 tubes of stuffed squid *(see point 7)*
100 g olive oil, 0.4° acidity
175 g onion
100 g carrot
75 g mature vine tomato
100 g white wine
5 g squid ink
750 g squid base *(see point 6)*
150 g fish stock *(see point 2)*
10 g cornflour (Maizena)
20 g mineral water
q.s. fine salt

❶ To clean the squid

Wash the squid in cold water. Pull the tentacles and remove all the viscera. Separate the tentacles from the eyes and set aside. Remove the squid skin and take off the fins, placing them to one side. Set the clean tentacles and fins aside for the stuffing. Turn the bodies over, remove the remaining viscera and set aside with the previous innards to prepare the stock. Put the squid in water to remove any remaining sand or viscera.
Drain, pat dry with paper towels and set aside in the fridge.

❷ For the fish stock

Soak the bones in a generous amount of iced water for 1 h to draw out the impurities and the blood.
Drain and place in a saucepan with water and salt, and cook on a low heat. When it begins to boil, allow to cook for 20 min and remove.
Once the stock is prepared, strain through a fine sieve and set aside.

❸ For the *sofrito*

Peel and thinly slice the garlic and sauté in the oil on a low heat without letting it brown.
Add the finely chopped onion, thyme, rosemary and bay leaves, and cook for 30 min on a very low heat until the onion begins to colour.
Peel the fresh tomato, remove the stem, dice into 1-cm cubes and add to the *sofrito*, leaving it on the heat until it begins to break down.
Add the chopped tomatoes and cook for 30 min. Add salt as necessary and set aside.

❹ To blanch the veal cheek

Soak the veal cheek for 1 h in a generous amount of iced water, then drain.
Mix the water, vinegar and salt in a saucepan.
Add the veal cheek and place on the heat. Once it begins to boil, allow to cook for 5 min. Drain and cool in iced water. Strain and separate the meat from the gelatin.
Cut each part into 5-mm cubes and mix 60% gelatin with 40% meat. Set aside in the fridge.

❺ For the squid stuffing

Sauté the squid tentacles and fins in a frying pan on a high heat, and set aside.
Place the *sofrito* on the heat, add the veal cheek and sautéd squid and cook for 5 min. Add the paprika and cook for an additional 5 min; then add the fish stock and the water, and reduce by half.
Cut the ham fat into 4-mm cubes and add to the stuffing. Add salt and pepper as necessary, and allow to cool.

❻ For the squid base

Sauté the chopped garlic and onion in a frying pan with oil. Add the chopped squid cuts, sauté and add a splash of white wine. Allow to reduce and add the water. Cook on a low heat for 30 min until a thick and flavoursome base is obtained; add salt as necessary.
Strain through a fine sieve and store in the fridge.

❼ To stuff the squid

Heat the stuffing to 70ºC so that it can be handled.
Take a squid tube with one hand, and with the other fill half the tube using a teaspoon.
Insert a round toothpick in the upper part, knitting the two sides together. Arrange the squid neatly on a platter.

❽ For the squid stew

Season the squid tubes with salt on all sides.
Put a frying pan with oil on a high heat and cook the squid until it turns golden, then set aside.
Peel and finely chop the onion and the carrot.
Peel the tomato and dice into 5-mm cubes.
Put the oil in a shallow saucepan on a low heat, add the vegetables and cook until it browns. Deglaze with white wine and allow to reduce until it is dry.
Dilute the squid ink in 50 g of fish stock and add, along with the remaining stock, to the stew.
Cover and allow to cook for 40 min on a low heat.
Once cooked, put the squid in a bowl and cover with the stock. Allow to cool.
Separate 500 g of ink sauce and bring it to the boil again to thicken.
Mix the cornflour and water using a whisk until smooth, and add to the boiling sauce. Allow to boil until the desired consistency is obtained. Season with salt and set aside.

Finishing and presentation

For each dish, cover 50 g of squid with the cooking liquid and heat on a low heat.
Check that it is hot on the inside by pinching it with a toothpick.
Heat 20 g of ink sauce. Arrange the hot squid in a line on the dish, having previously drained off the excess liquid.
Cover each squid with the ink sauce and serve.

MARKET FISH MARINATED IN MINI-SHIITAKE STEW

X 4

1 To clean the amberjack
1 medium-sized amberjack (sea bass, sea bream, gilt-head bream or corvina may also be used)

2 For the ginger oil
15 g fresh ginger
50 g sunflower oil

3 For the soy sauce base
140 g mineral water
10 g sugar
2 g granulated dashi
50 g soy sauce
2 g kombu

4 For the *sofrito* (sautéd garlic, onion and tomato base)
15 g garlic
50 g olive oil, 0.4° acidity
400 g onion
1 sprig thyme
1 sprig rosemary
2 bay leaves
80 g fresh tomato
20 g chopped tomatoes
q.s. fine salt

5 For the mushrooms confit
100 g mini-shiitake mushrooms
20 g *sofrito* *(see point 4)*
2 g fresh ginger
60 g soy sauce base *(see point 3)*
15 g garlic oil *(see point 2)*
25 g mineral water

6 To marinate the fish
q.s. clean amberjack *(see point 1)*
q.s. sauce to sauté the mushrooms *(see point 5)*

7 For the chive curls
q.s. fresh chives
q.s. mineral water
q.s. ice

Finishing and presentation
15 g mesclun of mini Asian sprouts

1 To clean the amberjack

Remove the scales and fillet the fish, trying to leave the fillet as whole as possible when removing the skin. Divide the fillet lengthwise into two parts.
Store in a container in the fridge.

2 For the ginger oil

Thinly slice the ginger with a knife. Sauté in a pan with sunflower oil for 30 min at 70ºC. Let it stand for 24 h and strain.

3 For the soy sauce base

Heat the water, sugar and granulated dashi.
Remove from the heat and add the soy sauce and kombu. Mix and set aside.

4 For the *sofrito*

Peel and thinly slice the garlic and sauté in the oil on a low heat without letting it brown.
Add the finely chopped onion, thyme, rosemary and bay leaves, and cook for 30 min on a very low heat until the onion begins to colour.
Peel the fresh tomato, remove the stem, dice into 1-cm cubes and add to the *sofrito*, leaving it on the heat until it begins to break down.
Add the chopped tomatoes and cook for 30 min. Add salt as necessary and set aside.

❺ For the mushrooms confit

Clean the mushrooms and remove the stem.
Heat the *sofrito* with the grated ginger.
Add the remaining ingredients and cook on a minimum heat for 20 min.
Strain and leave the mushrooms soaking in the liquid.

❻ To marinate the fish

Cut the amberjack into fillets 5 x 2 cm.
Marinate the fillets in the stock left over from sautéing the mushrooms, cold, for 2 min, before serving to the diners.

❼ For the chive curls

Cut the chives lengthwise as finely as possible and plunge into iced water to curl.

Finishing and presentation

Put 4 pieces of marinated fish on the dish and dress with the marinade. Garnish the fish with a few mini-shiitake mushrooms and finish with a scattering of chive curls and mesclun leaves.

SPICY TUNA BELLY TARTARE WITH CHERRIES

X 4

1 To clean the tuna belly
250 g tuna belly

2 For the xanthan base
160 g mineral water
1.6 g xanthan

3 For the spicy sauce
180 g kimchi
60 g soy sauce
60 g mirin
90 g rice vinegar
45 g xanthan base
(see point 2)

4 For the slices of pickled radish
60 g mineral water
2 g fine salt
8 g granulated sugar
12 g white wine vinegar
2 radishes

5 For the chive curls
q.s. fresh chives
q.s. mineral water
q.s. ice

Finishing and presentation
20 g virgin olive oil
1 lime
6 g toasted white sesame
4 cherries
4 g chives

❶ To clean the tuna belly

Separate the slices of tuna properly, following the partitions of the skin's tissue that is then discarded.
Dice into small cubes and set aside.

❷ For the xanthan base

Mix half the water with the xanthan.
Add the rest of the water and blend in a mixer until the xanthan has fully dissolved. Keep refrigerated at least overnight to eliminate the air bubbles.

❸ For the spicy sauce

Mix the kimchi, soy sauce, mirin and rice vinegar.
Add the xanthan base and mix with a whisk to the desired consistency.

❹ For the slices of pickled radish

Mix the water, sugar, salt and vinegar together, and stir with a whisk.
Cut the radishes into thin slices 1 mm thick with a mandolin.
Add the dressing to the sliced radishes, vacuum seal at 100% and set aside for 1 h.
Once this time has elapsed, open the bag, strain and set aside.
If you do not have a vacuum-sealing machine, *see page 170*.

❺ For the chive curls

Cut the chives lengthwise as finely as possible and plunge into iced water to curl.

Finishing and presentation

To prepare each dish, mix 60 g of tuna belly and 25 g of spicy sauce in a bowl.
Add 5 g of oil, the lime zest and a smidgen of toasted white sesame.
Arrange on the dish and garnish the tuna with 4 slices of radish, the cherry cut into quarters and the chive in the centre.

LLANGUETA WITH SEAWEED AND YUZU POWDER

X 4

❶ **For the fish**
200 g *llangueta* (Mediterranean blue fish)

❷ **For the soy sauce crystals**
250 g mineral water
15 g sugar
5 g granulated dashi
100 g soy sauce
5 g kombu
5 g xanthan

❸ **For the nori seaweed and soy powder**
30 g nori seaweed flakes
20 g soy sauce crystals
(see page 95)

❹ **For the egg**
4 eggs (50-60 g each)

Finishing and presentation
500 g plain wheat flour
920 g olive oil, 0.4° acidity
1 fresh yuzu
q.s. Maldon salt
q.s. fine salt

❶ **For the *llangueta***
Put the *llangueta* in a colander and rinse under running water to remove any impurities.
Drain and divide into 50-g portions on 4 paper towels.
Set aside in a container and refrigerate.

❷ **For the soy sauce crystals**
See page 95.

❸ **For the nori seaweed and soy powder**
Put both ingredients in a coffee grinder and grind to a fine powder. Set aside in a container in a dry place.

❹ **For the egg**
Separate the whites from the yolks. Place each yolk in individual cavities of a half-sphere silicone mould.
Cook in the oven (steam oven preferable) at 63°C for 22 min.
Cover with plastic wrap swiftly to prevent the yolks from drying out and allow to cool to room temperature.

Finishing and presentation
Put the fish in a colander and place in a bowl with cold water.
Drain off the excess water and roll loosely in the flour. Shake off the excess flour and cook in a deep-fat fryer at 190°C for 20 sec or until the fish is crisp.
Dry on paper towels, add salt as necessary and sprinkle with nori seaweed and soy powder.
Put the egg yolk on the dish and warm slightly under the grill.
Arrange the fried fish around the egg and grate yuzu zest over the top.
Season the egg yolk with Maldon salt as necessary and serve.

TUNA BELLY CONFIT IN TRADITIONAL PICKLING BRINE

X 4

1 For the tuna stock
1.6 kg tuna bones and cuts
50 g olive oil, 0.4° acidity
55 g white wine
1 kg mineral water
q.s. fine salt
1 g xanthan

2 For the tuna belly confit
500 g tuna belly
(320 g clean tuna belly)
200 g olive oil, 0.4° acidity
q.s. fine salt

3 For the pickling brine
70 g unpeeled garlic
160 g oil to confit the tuna
(see point 2)
3 g paprika
45 g white wine vinegar
5 g fresh rosemary
4 g fresh thyme
1 g granulated dashi
q.s. fine salt
220 g tuna stock *(see point 1)*

Finishing and presentation
1 g black peppercorns
1 bay leaf
1 garlic clove
1 sprig thyme

❶ For the tuna stock

Chop the tuna bones and cuts into pieces and brown in a frying pan with the oil. Add the white wine, reduce and add a splash of water.
Cook for 40 min, strain through a sieve and reduce to a thick and flavoursome stock (250 g of reduced stock should be obtained). Add salt as necessary and bind the stock with xanthan.
Set aside in the fridge.

❷ For the tuna belly confit

See next page.

❸ For the pickling brine

Sauté the crushed garlic cloves, unpeeled, in the oil at 70ºC.
Add the paprika and cook on a low heat without letting it burn.
Add the vinegar and leave for 5 min on the heat until it evaporates.
Off the heat, add all the herbs, the granulated dashi and the salt; let it infuse, covered with plastic wrap.
Once the pickling brine is cold, add the tuna stock.
Put the tuna belly confit in the pickling brine.
Set aside in the fridge.
Remove from the fridge 1 h before serving and allow to warm to room temperature.

Finishing and presentation

Put 4 pieces of slightly drained tuna belly on a paper towel.
Emulsify the pickling brine. Then dress the tuna belly with 50 g of pickling brine.
Garnish with a garlic clove, ½ a bay leaf and 1 sprig of thyme.
Finish with two turns of the pepper mill over the tuna.

TUNA BELLY CONFIT

Confit is a traditional Spanish cooking method. Thanks to this technique, perfect textures and cooking temperatures are obtained.

Separate the slices of tuna properly, following the partitions of the skin's tissue that is then discarded. Cut the tuna into uneven 5-cm pieces weighing 20 g. Generously season with salt.

1

Heat the oil to 90ºC.

2

Arrange the clean tuna belly on a dish and cover with freshly heated oil.

3

Confit for 10 min approx. and turn until it is medium rare. Remove the slices one by one as they cook and set aside. Set the oil aside.

4

AVOCADO AND BROWN CRAB CANNELLONE

X 4

1 For the brown crab filling
125 g brown crab meat
40 g brown crab coral
10 g chives
45 g sour cream
20 g mayonnaise
2 g Perrins sauce
1 g salt
q.s. black pepper

2 For the dill water
250 g mineral water
50 g dill

3 For the dill jelly
100 g dill water *(see point 2)*
1.2 g agar
1.5 g fine salt

4 For the roasted vegetables
420 g onion
1 head garlic (90 g)
250 g plum tomatoes
20 g olive oil, 0.4° acidity

5 For the *romesco* sauce
35 g roasted garlic
(see point 4)
80 g roasted plum tomato
(see point 4)
180 g roasted onion
(see point 4)
25 g ñora pepper flesh
60 g toasted hazelnuts
225 g olive oil, 0.4° acidity
8 g fine salt
20 g sherry vinegar
q.s. Tabasco sauce

6 For the avocado cannellone
4 avocados
q.s. brown crab filling
(see point 1)
q.s. *romesco* sauce
(see point 5)

Finishing and presentation
10 g Greek yoghurt
16 Atsina cress sprouts
12 chervil leaves
q.s. black pepper
q.s. extra virgin olive oil

❶ For the brown crab filling

Clean the brown crab meat carefully to remove any pieces of shell or cartilage. Chop the chives. Mix the brown crab meat with the remaining ingredients and set aside until the cannelloni are about to be made.

❷ For the dill water

Bring a saucepan of water to the boil. Remove the dill stalks, blanch and plunge into iced water to cool.
Blend the well-drained dill with cold water.
Strain through a sieve and set aside.

❸ For the dill jelly

Bring 50 g of dill water, with the agar and salt, to the boil.
Add the remaining dill water, mix and set aside in the fridge. Once the jelly is cold, blend to a very fine purée in a mixer.
Pour into a squeeze bottle and store in the fridge.

❹ For the roasted vegetables

Wrap the onion and garlic, drizzled with olive oil, in a piece of aluminium foil.
Heat the oven to 200°C. Roast the vegetables in the oven: the tomatoes for 20 min, the garlic for 30 min and the onion for 40 min.
Remove from the oven, allow to cool and peel. Set aside separately.

❺ For the *romesco* sauce

Mix all the ingredients together except for the oil and blend in a mixer or food processor.
Gradually add the oil until it forms a fine paste. Pour into a squeeze bottle and store in the fridge.

❻ For the avocado cannellone

See next page.

Finishing and presentation

Arrange the cannellone on the dish.
Put 4 dabs of Greek yoghurt along the cannellone, and in between each dab, a dab of dill jelly.
Garnish each dab of yoghurt with 1 Atsina cress sprout, and each dab of dill jelly with 1 chervil leaf.
Finish by sprinkling black pepper over the cannellone and dress with virgin olive oil.

Cut the avocado in two lengthwise. Separate the two halves, taking one half in one hand and twisting the other half in the opposite direction with the other hand.

1

Make avocado shavings 10 x 2 cm using a vegetable peeler. Brush parchment paper with olive oil.

2

ASSEMBLING THE AVOCADO CANNELLONE

Avocado and brown crab cannellone is one of Tickets' most successful dishes. Assembling the cannellone is perhaps one of the most difficult parts, but is manageable by following these simple guidelines.

Lay the shavings out on the paper, forming a slice 16 x 10 cm.

3

Fill each cannellone with 50 g of the crab meat mixture.

4

Dress the crab meat with 10 g of *romesco* sauce.

5

Wrap the cannellone in the same paper and set aside in the fridge until serving.

6

MUSSELS WITH TOMATO MARINIÈRE

X 4

1 To open the mussels
800 g mussels
q.s. mineral water
q.s. iced water

2 For the marinière sauce
5 g garlic
10 g olive oil, 0.4° acidity
20 g white wine
80 g chopped tomatoes
q.s. paprika
2 bay leaves
q.s. fine salt

3 For the *sofrito* (sautéd garlic, onion and tomato base)
15 g garlic
50 g olive oil, 0.4° acidity
400 g onion
1 sprig thyme
1 sprig rosemary
2 bay leaves
80 g fresh tomato
20 g chopped tomatoes
q.s. fine salt

4 For the tomato marinière
150 g marinière sauce *(see point 2)*
25 g *sofrito* *(see point 3)*
50 g mussel cooking liquid *(see point 1)*

5 For the mussel water
120 g mussel cooking liquid *(see point 1)*
0.2 g xanthan

Finishing and presentation
20 g chopped parsley

1 To open the mussels

Clean the mussels thoroughly. Wash them several times in cold water, removing the beards.
Cook the mussels for 10 sec in boiling water, just long enough for them to open. Plunge into iced water to cool. Remove one of the mussel shells.
Using the blade of a knife, cut the hinge muscle that joins the mussel to the shell and leave the mussel in the same shell.
Strain the mussel water through a sieve and set aside in the fridge.
Put the mussels in a container, covered with damp paper towels, and set aside in the fridge.

2 For the marinière sauce

Sauté the garlic and oil in a pan without letting it brown.
Add the white wine and reduce by half.
Add the chopped tomatoes, paprika and bay leaves, then cook for an additional 15 min.
Add salt as necessary and set aside.

3 For the *sofrito*

Peel and thinly slice the garlic and sauté in the oil on a low heat without letting it brown.
Add the finely chopped onion, thyme, rosemary and bay leaves, and cook for 30 min on a very low heat until the onion begins to colour.
Peel the fresh tomato, remove the stem, dice into 1-cm cubes and add to the *sofrito*, leaving it on the heat until it begins to break down.
Add the chopped tomatoes and cook for 30 min. Add salt as necessary and set aside.

4 For the tomato marinière

Mix all the ingredients together and cook for 7 min.
When the mussel water has reduced, strain.
Separate and chop the largest parts of the tomato.
Mix everything together again and refrigerate.
Once cold, divide into 65-g portions in plastic cups.

5 For the mussel water

Mix half the mussel water with the xanthan and blend in a mixer.
Add the remaining mussel water and mix again to the desired consistency. Store in a squeeze bottle in the fridge.

Finishing and presentation

In a pan, mix 65 g of marinière sauce and 30 g of mussel water, heat and allow to boil for 10 sec. Add the mussels, cover and remove from the heat.
Let it stand for 2 min. Warm the dishes, arrange the mussels on top and dress with the marinière sauce.
Sprinkle with chopped parsley and serve.

CLAMS WITH DUCK JUS SAUCE AND STAR ANISE

X 4

1 To open the clams
1 kg mineral water
15 g fine salt
500 g large Carril clams

2 For the garlic chips
10 g garlic
50 g olive oil, 0.4° acidity

3 For the duck stock
(minimum quantity for a good result)
500 g clean and eviscerated duck
50 g olive oil, 0.4° acidity
50 g onion
60 g white wine
500 g mineral water

4 For the *sofrito* (sautéd garlic, onion and tomato base)
15 g garlic
50 g olive oil, 0.4° acidity
400 g onion
1 sprig thyme
1 sprig rosemary
2 bay leaves
80 g fresh tomato
20 g chopped tomatoes
q.s. fine salt

5 For the star anise oil
30 g star anise
200 g sunflower oil

6 For the xanthan base
160 g mineral water
2 g xanthan

7 For the duck sauce
150 g duck stock *(see point 3)*
100 g star anise oil *(see point 5)*
15 g ***sofrito*** *(see point 4)*
15 g Jang Korean soy sauce
12 g xanthan base *(see point 6)*

Finishing and presentation
100 g duck stock *(see point 3)*
q.s. duck sauce *(see point 7)*
50 g coarse salt
20 clam shells
15 g toasted white sesame
q.s. garlic chips *(see point 2)*
20 Atsina cress sprouts

❶ To open the clams
Bring salted water to the boil. Blanch the clams for 5 sec and plunge into iced water to cool. Using a knife, open the clam, cut the hinge muscle that joins it to the shell and store in a container. Set the shells aside for the dish presentation later on.
Retain any liquid released to cover the meat and prevent it from drying out. Set aside in the fridge.

❷ For the garlic chips
Peel and cut the garlic gloves into thin slices 1 mm thick. Sauté the sliced garlic in oil in a frying pan until it begins to brown.
Remove from the heat, strain and dry on paper towels.

❸ For the duck stock
Cut the duck into cubes 3 cm thick.
Put half the oil in a pan on a low heat and brown lightly on both sides.
Remove the duck and add the rest of the oil and diced 3-cm onion cubes, and allow to brown. Add the duck, turn up the heat, add a splash of white wine and allow to reduce until it evaporates. Cover with water and allow to cook for 25 min. Stain through a sieve and set aside in the fridge for 12 h. Remove the fat on the surface and reduce the stock to a flavoursome jus.

❹ For the *sofrito*
Peel and thinly slice the garlic and sauté in the oil on a low heat without letting it brown.
Add the finely chopped onion, thyme, rosemary and bay leaves, and cook for 30 min on a very low heat until the onion begins to colour.
Peel the fresh tomato, remove the stem, dice into 1-cm cubes and add to the *sofrito*, leaving it on the heat until it begins to break down.
Add the chopped tomatoes and cook for 30 min. Add salt as necessary and set aside.

❺ For the star anise oil
Break the star anise into pieces. Put it in a pan with the sunflower oil on a minimum heat for 10 min. Remove from the heat and let it infuse for an additional 10 min. Strain and set aside.

❻ For the xanthan base
Mix half the water with the xanthan. Add the rest of the water and blend in a mixer until the xanthan has fully dissolved. Remove the air in a vacuum-sealing machine (or *see page 170*) and set aside.

❼ For the duck sauce
Mix all the ingredients in a pan, bring to the boil and set aside.

Finishing and presentation
Heat the stock and duck sauce. Lay a bed of coarse salt on a dish, arrange 5 clam shells on top and warm under the grill. Remove the duck stock from the heat and add the clams for 10 sec.
Put the clams in the shells and dress each clam with 8 g of duck sauce. Warm under the grill, arrange on a dish and finish with the sesame, the garlic chips and an Atsina sprout on each clam.

PRAWNS MARINATED IN SOY SAUCE AND GINGER

X 4

1 For the soy sauce and ginger marinade
100 g mineral water
6 g star anise
12 g ginger
80 g soy sauce

2 For the soy sauce base
140 g mineral water
60 g soy sauce
12 g ginger
0.2 g xanthan

3 To peel the prawns
400 g prawns

4 For the Codium seaweed juice
100 g mineral water
q.s. salt
100 g Codium seaweed
q.s. iced water

5 For the parsley and Codium dressing
12 g parsley
12 g Codium seaweed juice *(see point 4)*
40 g extra virgin olive oil
q.s. fine salt

Finishing and presentation
1 orange
q.s. extra virgin olive oil

1 For the soy sauce and ginger marinade

Boil the water with the star anise and allow to infuse off the heat for 20 min. Remove the anise and set aside.
Grate the ginger and add to the water along with the soy sauce.
Strain, pressing the ginger to release all its juices, and add the star anise again. Set aside in the fridge.

2 For the soy sauce base

Mix the water and soy sauce, and grate the ginger.
Strain, pressing the ginger to release all its juices. Blend the liquid and the xanthan in a mixer. Store in a squeeze bottle in the fridge for 24 h.

3 To peel the prawns

Remove the prawns' whiskery antennae. Peel the prawns removing just the belly and leaving part of the shell at the head and tail ends. Set aside in the fridge.

4 For the Codium seaweed juice

Bring salted water to the boil (36 g salt per litre of water).
Blanch the seaweed for 10 sec.
Plunge into iced salted water (15 g salt per litre) to cool.
Blend the Codium seaweed in an equal quantity of cooling water.
Strain the juice obtained through a coarse sieve and set aside.

5 For the parsley and Codium dressing

Mix all the ingredients together, blend in a mixer and set aside.

Finishing and presentation

Marinate the prawns in the soy sauce and ginger marinade for 8 min.
Remove, line up in a dish and warm under the grill for just 30 sec to prevent overcooking.
Turn the prawns over and dress with a little soy sauce base.
Warm again for 20 sec under the grill and remove. They should be warm but a little raw.
Arrange neatly on a dish and dress with the prawn cooking liquid.
Add a dab of parsley and Codium dressing to the head of each prawn and lightly grate orange zest over the body.
Just before serving, drizzle with a splash of olive oil.

PRAWNS WITH LAPSANG SOUCHONG BLACK TEA SALT

X 4

1 For the prawns
4 fresh red prawns
(50 g approx./unit)

2 For the black tea infusion
80 g mineral water
4 g Lapsang Souchong
black tea

3 For the black tea and soy sauce base
170 g mineral water
0.3 g xanthan
60 g soy sauce
40 g black tea infusion
(see point 2)

4 For the black tea salt
4 g Lapsang Souchong
black tea
500 g coarse salt
30 g mineral water

1 For the prawns

Choose prawns that are well closed where the head meets the body to prevent any liquid from escaping.
Wash the prawns and remove the whiskery antennae. Set aside in the fridge between damp paper towels.

2 For the black tea infusion

Heat the water to 95ºC, and once removed from the heat, add the black tea.
Cover and allow to infuse for 5 min, then strain and set aside.

3 For the black tea and soy sauce base

Blend the liquid and the xanthan in a mixer.
Add the remaining ingredients, mix and remove the air in a vacuum-sealing machine. If you do not have a vacuum-sealing machine, *see page 170*. Set aside at room temperature.

4 For the black tea salt

Grind the black tea to a fine powder in a coffee grinder.
Mix the black tea powder with the coarse salt and add the mineral water.
Mix and set aside at room temperature.

Finishing and presentation

Preheat the oven to 180ºC.
On a deep tray, lay a bed of the coarse salt and black tea mixture and arrange the prawns separately on top.
Cover with the rest of the coarse salt without leaving any parts of the prawn exposed.
Bake in the oven for 6 min 30 sec.
Remove the tray from the oven.
Break and remove the layer of salt at the tableside.
Remove the prawns from the tray, as well as any excess salt.
Serve on a dish with the black tea and soy sauce separately.

COD *SANFAINA* GARNISHED WITH A LARGE COD CRACKER

X 4

❶ **For the *sanfaina* (variation of ratatouille)**
400 g aubergine
400 g onion
1 garlic clove
120 g tomato
20 g olive oil, 0.4° acidity
15 g white wine
q.s. salt

❷ **For the cod**
250 g desalted cod tail

❸ **For the cod powder**
300 g desalted cod tail

❹ **For the cod cracker**
1 round rice cracker
q.s. egg white
20 g cod powder *(see point 3)*
q.s. sunflower oil

Finishing and presentation
q.s. chives

❶ For the *sanfaina*

Peel and cut the aubergine into triangular 2-cm pieces.
Peel and dice the onion into 1-cm cubes. Peel and mince the garlic. Peel and chop the tomato.
Fry the onion and aubergine separately in a deep-fat fryer at 125°C for 10 min.
Sauté the garlic in olive oil in a pan.
Add the tomato, sauté for 5 min and add the fried onion. Then add a splash of white wine and reduce. Add the fried aubergine. Cook for 15 min on a low heat, add salt as necessary and remove from the heat.
Once cold, set aside 100 g of *sanfaina* per person and store in the fridge.

❷ For the cod

Test the saltiness of the cod.
Remove the skin, which will be used to make the cod powder.
Cut the cod into rectangles 1.5 x 2 cm approx.
Set aside 50 g of cod per person and store in the fridge.

❸ For the cod powder

Remove the scales from the cod.
Remove the skin and lay on baking parchment.
Blend the cod flesh in a mixer to form a paste. Using a rolling pin, roll the cod paste out between baking parchment and a piece of plastic wrap to a thickness of 2 to 3 mm.
Remove the plastic wrap and blast in the oven at 140°C to prevent possible fermentation.
Dry the cod paste and skins in the oven at 90°C for 6 or 8 h.
Once dry, blend both to an uneven powder in a mixer. Set aside.

❹ For the cod cracker

Brush the rice cracker with the egg white, not excessively.
Sprinkle over the cod powder and allow to dry for about 12 h.
Fry the cracker in oil at 180°C until it inflates. Drain and dry off the excess oil on absorbent paper towels.

Finishing and presentation

Put 100 g of *sanfaina* in a pan with a little water. Heat until it reaches 80°C.
Add the cod and remove from the heat. Mix carefully to prevent breaking the cod.
Arrange the cod in a dish, and finish with a little chopped chive on top. Serve the large cod cracker separately. It is suggested that the diner spread the sanfaina on top of the cod cracker for tasting.

LAS TAPAS DE LA TIERRA

MARESME PEAS SEASONED WITH MINT *EN PAPILLOTE*

X 4

1 For the blanched peas
320 g fresh peas
q.s. mineral water

2 For the pea juice
120 g frozen peas
120 g mineral water
q.s. fine salt

3 For the diced pancetta
60 g pancetta

4 For the diced Iberian ham
30 g Iberian ham (Joselito)

5 For the *sofrito* (sautéd garlic, onion and tomato base)
15 g garlic
50 g olive oil, 0.4° acidity
400 g onion
1 sprig thyme
1 sprig rosemary
2 bay leaves
80 g fresh tomato
20 g chopped tomatoes
q.s. fine salt

6 For the *papillote* of peas seasoned with mint
120 g pea juice *(see point 2)*
20 g mineral water
320 g blanched peas *(see point 1)*
40 g *sofrito* *(see point 5)*
28 g diced pancetta *(see point 3)*
28 g Iberian ham *(see point 4)*
32 g black butifarra sausage
q.s. dry anise liqueur
½ bunch mint
q.s. salt
q.s. black pepper

1 For the blanched peas
Bring water to the boil and blanch the peas for 50 sec to 1 min, then plunge rapidly into iced water to cool.

2 For the pea juice
Boil the water, and when it reaches boiling point, add the frozen peas and remove immediately from the heat. Blend in a mixer, strain through a mesh colander and add salt as necessary.
Store refrigerated.

3 For the diced pancetta
Cut the pancetta in the meat-slicing machine to a thickness of 3 mm. Remove the outer rind and dice the pancetta into 3-mm cubes.

4 For the diced Iberian ham
Dice the ham into 3-mm cubes and set aside.

5 For the *sofrito*
Peel and thinly slice the garlic and sauté in the oil on a low heat without letting it brown.
Add the finely chopped onion, thyme, rosemary and bay leaves, and cook for 30 min on a very low heat until the onion begins to colour.
Peel the fresh tomato, remove the stem, dice into 1-cm cubes and add to the *sofrito*, leaving it on the heat until it begins to break down.
Add the chopped tomatoes and cook for 30 min. Add salt as necessary and set aside.

6 For the *papillote* of peas seasoned with mint
See page 139.

Finishing and presentation
Serve the *papillote* on a very hot platter to prevent heat loss and the bag from deflating.
Open the *papillote* at the tableside with scissors, removing the mint as the idea is for the herb to simply imbue the dish with its aroma.

To select peas of the same size, a plastic tray and a drill will suffice.

1

Drill holes in the bottom of the tray with a conical 5-mm bit.

2

PEAS OF THE SAME SIZE

To prepare this recipe, small peas are used. However, the same pod may contain peas of a different size. By following this simple tip, peas of the ideal size can be selected while the others can be set aside for other dishes.

Spread the shelled peas on the tray pierced with holes.

3

Shake the tray. The peas that fall through the holes will be used in this recipe.

4

Place 4 clear sheets of parchment suitable for cooking (Carta Fata), cut into 60 x 50 cm pieces, in a slightly concave dish.

1

In each *papillote*, place the following ingredients in this order: 30 g of pea juice, 5 g of mineral water, 80 g of blanched peas and 8 g of *sofrito*.

2

PREPARING THE *PAPILLOTE*

Cooking *en papillote* means the food is cooked in its own juices and the steam given off. In the case of the peas in this recipe, the ingredients prepared in this manner retain the intensity of their flavour and colour. Using this technique, very tasty dishes can be prepared in a relatively short time.

Continue with 7 g of diced pancetta, 7 g of diced ham, 6 g of butifarra sausage and 3 drops of dry anise liqueur (using a pipette).

3

Finally, add 2 sprigs of fresh mint 5 cm long, salt and freshly ground black pepper.

4

Fold the sheet edges inwards, tying them together to form a bundle, tightly fastening with the accompanying string. Set aside in the fridge.

5

Just before serving the dish, place the papillote in a frying pan on a medium heat and cook for 3 min, until the contents of the papillote have begun to boil.

6

WOK OF SAUTÉD WHITE BEANS, IBERIAN PORK SAUSAGES AND BABY CUTTLEFISH

X 4

1 For the Iberian pork sausages
320 g Iberian pork sausage

2 For the rib juice
1.5 kg pork rib
8 g garlic
50 g onion
40 g red wine
400 g mineral water
q.s. salt

3 For the ham stock
100 g ham cuts
500 g mineral water
500 g ham bones

4 For the rib and ham gravy
150 g rib juice *(see point 2)*
50 g ham stock *(see point 3)*
25 g mineral water
q.s. xanthan

5 To clean the baby cuttlefish
200 g fresh baby cuttlefish

6 For the *sofrito* (sautéd garlic, onion and tomato base)
15 g garlic
50 g olive oil, 0.4° acidity
400 g onion
1 sprig thyme
1 sprig rosemary
2 bay leaves
80 g fresh tomato
20 g chopped tomatoes
q.s. fine salt

Finishing and presentation
10 g chopped parsley
320 g cooked Santa Pau white beans
60 g olive oil, 0.4° acidity
q.s. extra virgin olive oil

❶ For the Iberian pork sausages
Cut the sausages in 7-g pieces (7 per serving).

❷ For the rib juice
In a frying pan, sear the pork rib, previously cut into 3-cm pieces and seasoned with salt, on all sides. Add the crushed garlic cloves and sauté. Add the onion cut into julienne strips and sauté. Deglaze with red wine and reduce. Add the mineral water and allow to cook gently to extract the juices and to let the water evaporate gradually.

❸ For the ham stock
Chop the ham cuts and add to the water and the bones.
Cook on a low heat for 1 h and strain.
Strain the consommé obtained through paper towels.

❹ For the rib and ham gravy
Mix the rib juice, the ham stock and water in a pan.
Bind with the xanthan in a mixer to the desired consistency and set aside.

❺ To clean the baby cuttlefish
Remove the cuttlebone carefully so as not to break the intestinal sac. Using scissors, remove the mouth and the eyes. Rinse with water to remove any possible grit and dry on paper towels.
Cut out pieces of baking parchment measuring 8 x 5 cm to wrap 50-g portions of baby cuttlefish. Set aside in the fridge.

❻ For the *sofrito*
Peel and thinly slice the garlic and sauté in the oil on a low heat without letting it brown.
Add the finely chopped onion, thyme, rosemary and bay leaves, and cook for 30 min on a very low heat until the onion begins to colour.
Peel the fresh tomato, remove the stem, dice into 1-cm cubes and add to the *sofrito*, leaving it on the heat until it begins to break down.
Add the chopped tomatoes and cook for 30 min.
Add salt as necessary and set aside.

Finishing and presentation
See next page.

Select all the ingredients prepared earlier.

1

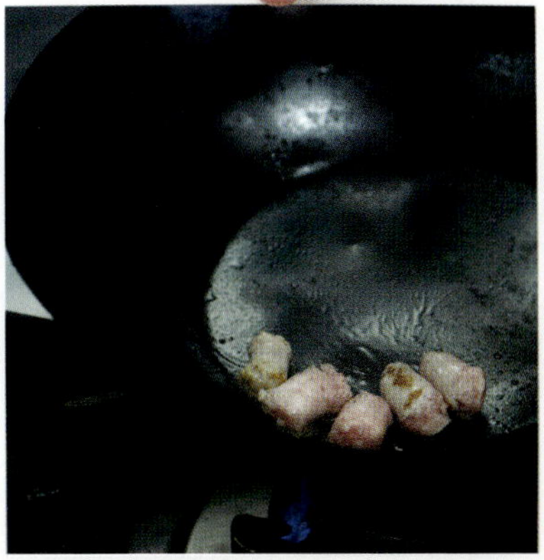

Place the wok on a high heat with 15 g of oil, and when it begins to smoke, add 7 pieces of sausage until they brown.

2

WOK COOKING

The wok, a frying pan originating from China, allows stir-fries to be made instantly. Thanks to its wide shape, the heat is distributed evenly, thereby reducing the food's cooking time. Without a doubt, wok cooking is one of the features of the future cuisine at Tickets.

Sauté the white beans with the sausages and add 10 g of *sofrito* and 2 g of parsley.

3

Deglaze with 25 g of the pork rib and ham gravy.

4

Season the baby cuttlefish and braise them in the preheated wok on a high heat. Allow them to brown and remove when cooked.

5

Serve the stir-fry on the dish and arrange the sausages around it. Arrange the baby cuttlefish in between the sausages and add any juice they released. Finish with a drizzle of extra virgin olive oil.

6

ROAST BEEF GARNISHED WITH POTATOES

X 4

1 For the roast beef
200 g veal tenderloin
200 g fine salt
10 g sugar
0.8 g dill
0.8 g cardamom
1 g red pepper
1 g Jamaican pepper
0.8 g star anise

2 For the meat stock
100 g red wine
4 g sugar
100 g veal shank bones
100 g blanquette of veal
10 g olive oil, 0.4° acidity
35 g onion
15 g carrot
15 g leek
10 g mature red tomato
250 g mineral water

3 For the bacon oil
30 g smoked bacon
50 g sunflower oil

4 For the mustard mayonnaise
60 g mayonnaise
40 g Dijon mustard

5 For the potato brunoise
100 g Agria potato

6 For the meat gravy
70 g meat stock *(see point 2)*
30 g tonkatsu sauce

Finishing and presentation
16 micro rocket leaves
16 capers
q.s. fine salt

1 For the roast beef

Remove the chain and any sinew from the tenderloin.
Mix the salt, sugar and spices.
Put the tenderloin in a vacuum bag with the previous mixture ensuring it is well covered, remove the air in a vacuum-sealing machine (or *see page 170*) and store in the fridge for 8 h.
Once this time has elapsed, wash, dry and cut the tenderloin into 10-cm pieces, and sear in a frying pan on both sides.
Smoke the tenderloin with a smoking gun for 15 min.
Wrap in plastic wrap and freeze for 15 min for the meat to become more solid.
When it is semi-frozen, cut using a meat-slicing machine to a thickness of 3.5 mm and set the portions aside, individually wrapped in plastic wrap.

2 For the meat stock

Mix the red wine with the sugar and put on the heat until it reduces by half. Set aside to deglaze the frying pan where the blanquette will be seared.
Put the veal bones in the oven at 180°C.
Cut the blanquette into pieces 10 cm x 1.5 cm. Sear in a frying pan with a little oil on a high heat, until golden but rare on the inside. Deglaze with the previously reduced wine.
Chop the vegetables into small pieces. Brown in the oven with a little oil at 150°C.
Once they begin to brown evenly, add the tomato cut into eighths. Continue cooking until the tomato has lost its water and the mixture displays a toasted colour.
Mix all the ingredients together in a saucepan. Cover with cold water and place on a medium heat.
Once it begins to boil, lower the heat so that it simmers for 6 h. Skim off the fat at regular intervals. Strain and allow to cool so that the fat solidifies. Remove the fat. Then reduce the meat stock to a third.

3 For the bacon oil

Dice the smoked bacon into 5-mm cubes.
Put the oil and bacon in a pan on a low heat and brown until the bacon is crisp. Remove from the heat and allow to cool, straining it to remove the excess fat. Set aside.

4 For the mustard mayonnaise

Mix the two ingredients and set aside in a piping bag.

5 For the potato brunoise

Peel the potato.
Thinly slice to a thickness of 3.5 mm using a meat-slicing machine or a mandolin.
Cut with a knife into strips 2 mm thick and then dice into 2 x 2-mm cubes. Dry well with parchment paper.
Put in a heat-resistant mesh basket and fry in a pan, basket included, with the oil at 120°C,

until crisp. Drain on paper towels and season with salt.
Put in the oven on parchment paper at 100ºC for 8 min, until they lose all their moisture.

❻ For the meat gravy
Mix the two ingredients and set aside.

Finishing and presentation
Arrange 4 slices of roast beef on each dish.
Season with salt if necessary and dress each slice with the meat gravy.
Put a dab of mustard mayonnaise on the upper left-hand side of each slice. Then garnish the mayonnaise with a caper and a micro rocket leaf.
Drizzle two drops of bacon oil on each slice of meat and garnish the centre with the diced potatoes.

ROAST CHICKEN CANAPÉ

X 4

❶ For the chicken canapé
200 g chicken skin
q.s. dried rosemary
q.s. chicken spice mix

❷ For the chicken juice
(minimum quantity for a good result)
650 g chicken wings
25 g carrot
25 g onion
12 g leek
12 g celery
75 g white wine
250 g chicken stock
q.s. olive oil, 0.4° acidity
250 g mineral water

❸ For the garlic oil
80 g olive oil, 0.4° acidity
4 garlic cloves

❹ For the chicken in pickling brine
120 g chicken juice *(see point 2)*
20 g sherry vinegar
20 g garlic oil *(see point 3)*
0.4 g xanthan
q.s. fine salt

❺ To cook the chicken breast
160 g chicken breast
q.s. salt
q.s. black pepper
q.s. olive oil

Finishing and presentation
1 lemon
q.s. black pepper

❶ For the chicken canapé

Remove the excess fat from the chicken skin.
Put the chicken skin on a tray lined with parchment paper and leave covered in the freezer for 12 h.
Defrost and season the skin with salt and pepper to enhance its flavour.
Put the chicken skin on a rack, cover with parchment paper and place another rack on top to prevent it from curling. Bake in the oven at 180°C for 20 min. Then, lower the temperature to 160°C and allow to cook for 20 min. After that, remove the rack and the parchment paper and leave for an additional 5 min. Lower the temperature to 120°C and leave for 20 min, but in the last 5 min, sprinkle dried rosemary and chicken spices on top.
Once out of the oven and crisp, cut the skin using scissors, into slightly triangular pieces 5 cm on each side.
Set aside in a container in a cool and dry place.

❷ For the chicken juice

In a pan, fry the chicken wings in oil and remove when golden.
Add the onion and carrot cut into thin julienne strips.
When the onion and the carrot have browned, add the celery and leek and allow to cook. Add the chicken wings and caramelise.
Add the wine, allow all the alcohol to evaporate, add the chicken stock and water, and cook for 35 min.
Strain through a sieve and allow to cool in a tall container to allow the fat to be poured off easily.
Heat the chicken juice and allow to reduce by a third.

❸ For the garlic oil

Crush the garlic and sauté on a low heat for 10 min.
When the garlic has softened, remove the oil from the heat and set aside.

❹ For the chicken in pickling brine

Dissolve the xanthan in the chicken juice using a mixer.
Season with salt as necessary and add the vinegar. Boil for 1 min to fully incorporate the flavours. Add the garlic oil and cook for an additional 2 min.

❺ To cook the chicken breast

Season the chicken breasts with salt and pepper and sear on both sides in a frying pan with a little oil.
Bake at 180°C with a probe thermometer to check when it reaches 54°C on the inside and remove.
Set aside at room temperature.

Finishing and presentation

Cut the chicken breast into slices 2 mm thick and, on top of each piece of chicken skin, arrange 4 of these slices in a slightly wavy manner, covering the base.
Warm gently under the grill or in an oven and dress with the hot chicken pickling brine.
Finish by grinding two turns of the black pepper mill over the chicken and a sprinkle of grated lemon zest.

41º NORDIC LANDSCAPE

X 4

1 To clean the tenderloin
450 g beef tenderloin
(300 g clean tenderloin)

2 To marinate the tenderloin
7 g dill
7 g pink pepper
7 g Jamaican pepper
1.2 g star anise
1.2 g cardamom seeds
500 g coarse salt
250 g granulated sugar
300 g clean tenderloin
(see point 1)

3 For the clarified butter
100 g butter

4 For the malt bread
500 g sliced malt bread
20 g clarified butter
(see point 3)
q.s. fine salt

5 For the pickled shallot
50 g shallot
50 g apple vinegar
35 g rosemary honey
30 g mineral water
1 g black peppercorns
1 g fresh thyme

6 For the pickled red onion
30 g red onion
4 g dried bay leaf
4 g black peppercorns
40 g apple vinegar
40 g sugar
40 g mineral water

7 For the smoked cheese
125 g cream cheese
40 g sour cream
q.s. fine salt
q.s. black peppercorns

8 For the vinegar snow
20 g maltodextrin (Malt)
30 g vinegar powder

Finishing and presentation
10 g soy sauce
20 fresh dill sprigs
q.s. black peppercorns
q.s. olive oil

❶ To clean the tenderloin

Remove the excess fat and sinew from the tenderloin, leaving the meat as clean and full as possible. Set aside to marinate.

❷ To marinate the tenderloin

Mix all the spices together and toast in a frying pan on the heat. Put the toasted spices in a mixer or food processor and blend for 5 sec without crushing them entirely. Mix the toasted spices with salt and sugar.
Lay a bed with part of the above mixture in a vacuum bag, put the tenderloin in the centre and cover with the rest of the salt and spices.
Remove 60% of the air in a vacuum-sealing machine and set aside in the fridge for 4 h 30 min. If you do not have a vacuum-sealing machine, *see page 170*. Remove the tenderloin and rinse under running water to remove the excess salt.
Dry on paper towels. Roll the tenderloin in plastic wrap, into a tube-like shape, and place in the freezer for 12 h.
Remove the tenderloin from the freezer and, after letting it stand at room temperature for 1 h, dice into 4-mm cubes. Some 80 g of meat are needed per diner. Bear in mind that the meat loses 5% of its weight in the marinade.
Store in a container in the fridge.

❸ For the clarified butter

Melt the butter and let it stand. Separate the whey from the fat, which will gradually rise to the surface. Discard using a spoon and finally strain through a sieve. Set the clarified butter aside.

❹ For the malt bread

Cut off the crusts. Cut in half, wrap in plastic wrap and freeze. Cut the frozen pieces of bread with a meat-slicing machine to a thickness of 4.5 cm. Slices 10 x 4.5 x 5 cm will therefore be obtained.
Lightly butter the pieces of bread and add salt.
Put the slices of bread between two sheets of silicone (Silipat) and bake at 170°C for 15 min until they are fully crisp. Allow to cool.
Store in a container with packets of silica gel to absorb any moisture.

❺ For the pickled shallot

Peel the shallots and cut them in half lengthwise.
Mix the remaining ingredients and put in a frying pan on a low heat until they begin to boil.
Add the shallots and continue on the heat for 3 min.
Remove from the heat and let it stand for 12 h in the fridge.

❻ For the pickled red onion

Peel the onion and select the thickest layers. Cut the layers in half crosswise. Then cut vertical 3-mm strips.
Mix the bay leaf, pepper, apple vinegar, sugar and water together. Put the previous mixture in a pan on a medium heat and allow to infuse for a few minutes. Add the onion and let it stand for 12 h in the fridge.

❼ For the smoked cheese

Mix the cheese with the sour cream and blend in a mixer until smooth.
Smoke the cheese with a smoking gun for 15 min. Season with salt and pepper and put the cheese in a plastic piping bag. Set aside in the fridge.
When using, cut the top to a thickness of 3 mm.

❽ For the vinegar snow

Mix the maltodextrin and the vinegar.
Store in a container.

Finishing and presentation

Put 3 dollops of smoked cheese on each piece of toasted malt bread.
Dress 20 g of meat with the olive oil, soy sauce and black pepper, and place on the toasted bread without covering the cheese.
Put 1 slice of shallot in the centre of the toast and 2 strips of onion on the ends.
Put 4 sprigs of fresh dill on top of the cheese and the meat.
To finish, garnish with the vinegar snow and serve.

FRIED CHICKEN'S EGG WITH TRUFFLED DUCK FAT AND POTATO CREAM

X 4

❶ For the boiled potatoes
350 g Red Pontiac potatoes
q.s. mineral water
1 bay leaf
5 black peppercorns

❷ For the potato cream
280 g boiled potatoes *(see point 1)*
60 g potato cooking liquid *(see point 1)*
120 g cream, 35% fat
30 g olive oil, 0.4° acidity
q.s. fine salt

❸ For the duck fat with black truffle
10 g black truffle
50 g duck fat

❹ For the fried eggs
8 eggs
60 g olive oil, 0.4° acidity

❺ For the egg and truffle mixture
8 fried eggs (80 g fried egg yolk and 40 g fried egg white)
25 g pasteurised yolk
20 g duck fat with black truffle *(see point 3)*
q.s. fine salt
q.s. ground black pepper

❻ To fill the eggs
4 egg shells to fill
40 g egg and truffle mixture *(see point 5)*

❼ For the black truffle purée
15 g black truffle
20 g olive oil, 0.4° acidity

Finishing and presentation
200 g coarse salt

❶ For the boiled potatoes
Peel and chop the potatoes. Pour cold water into a saucepan, add the potatoes with the pepper and bay leaf and cook for 20 min. Set aside the potatoes and the water.

❷ For the potato cream
Put the cooked potato in a mixer with the cooking liquid, cream and oil, and blend at medium speed.
Add salt as necessary and strain.
Put the potato cream in a ½-litre siphon and close, adding 3 gas cartridges.

❸ For the duck fat with black truffle
Brush away any dirt clinging to the truffle with the help of a little water.
Warm up the duck fat until it liquefies.
Add the truffle and blend in a mixer to obtain a truffle purée.
Place in a bag for sous-vide cooking. Cook in a bain marie using a Roner at 63°C for 2 h.
Remove and let it stand. If you do not have a Roner, *see page 170*.

❹ For the fried eggs
Heat the oil in a frying pan; when it begins to smoke, fry the eggs. Set aside.

❺ For the egg and truffle mixture
Chop up the white, break the egg yolk with a knife and place in a bowl.
Using a knife, dice the white into small cubes and mix with the yolk.
Add the remaining ingredients and mix again.

❻ To fill the eggs
Fill the eggs with 10 g of the egg and truffle mixture. Wrap each egg individually in plastic wrap and store in the fridge.

❼ For the black truffle purée
Cut the truffle into 3-cm pieces and mix with the oil. Blend in a mixer. Set aside in the fridge and remove just before serving.

Finishing and presentation
Remove the eggs from the fridge and put in a preheated oven at 80°C (preferably a steam oven) for 2 min in an egg box covered with aluminium foil.
Once hot, fill the shell up to the edge with potato cream foam.
In the centre of the egg, put 0.5 g of black truffle purée and serve.

PORK JOWL BUN

X 4

1 For the brioche dough
250 g flour
75 g butter
80 g full-fat milk
10 g compressed fresh yeast
20 g sugar
90 g whole egg
5 g salt

2 For the brioche
q.s. brioche dough
(see point 1)

3 For the pork jowl confit
2 g paprika
2 g cayenne pepper
1 g ras el hanout
1.5 g salt
300 g fresh pork jowl
q.s. olive oil

4 For the bun filling
150 g pork jowl confit
(see point 3)
150 g crackling pork
(El Mantecas)

5 For the soy sauce and water mixture
50 g Jang Korean soy sauce
150 g mineral water

6 For the mozzarella cream
125 g mozzarella

Finishing and presentation
50 g Dijon mustard

1 For the brioche dough

Pour the flour into a kneading machine with the dough hook.
Soften the butter at room temperature.
Heat the milk to 37ºC and add the sugar and yeast.
Run the kneading machine at minimum speed and gradually add the milk mixture to the flour. Next, gradually add the butter and, finally, the beaten egg, also bit by bit.
Turn up the speed of the machine. When the dough begins to have a smooth consistency, add the salt. Knead for an additional 5 min and remove from the machine. Set the dough aside wrapped in plastic wrap in the fridge for 24 h.

2 For the brioche

Divide the dough into 150-g portions and roll out manually into strips of dough 2 cm thick. Using a knife, divide the dough into 17-g portions.
Roll the dough into balls and place on a tray lined with parchment paper. Allow the brioche dough to ferment for 50 or 60 min.
Cook the brioche in the oven at 94ºC (in the case of a steam oven, set at 100% humidity and the fan at medium power) for 15 min.
Cool the brioche to room temperature and store in a container in the fridge.

3 For the pork jowl confit

Mix the spices and the salt.
Smear the spice mixture over the pork jowl and pack in a vacuum bag with a drizzle of oil.
Cook in the oven (steam oven preferable) at 75ºC for 12 h. If you do not have a vacuum-sealing machine, *see page 170*. Remove from the oven, plunge into iced water, and set aside in the fridge.

4 For the bun filling

Slice the pork jowl and the crackling pork in a meat-slicing machine, making 15-mm slices, weighing 5 g. Prepare servings of 2 slices of pork jowl and 1 slice of crackling pork in between.
Store wrapped in parchment paper and refrigerate.

5 For the soy sauce and water mixture

Mix the soy sauce and water, pour into a squeeze bottle and set aside in the fridge.

6 For the mozzarella cream

Open the mozzarella and keep the whey from one packet.
Blend the mozzarella in a mixer with 20 g of its whey to a thick and fine cream.
Store in a container in the fridge.

Finishing and presentation
Cut open the brioche horizontally. Put a spoonful of the soy sauce mixture in a frying pan, add the bun filling and cook slightly until hot. Cover the base of the brioche with the mozzarella cream and arrange 2 pieces of hot pork jowl on top. Dress the pork jowl with 1.5 g of Dijon mustard. Close the brioche and cook in a sandwich toaster for 20 sec, so that the brioche is hot and toasted on the outside. Serve
on a tray with baking parchment.

PAYOYO CHEESE, TRADITION AND EVOLUTION

X 4

1 For the lemon jam
100 g lemon
50 g sugar
10 g glucose

2 To prepare the bread
¼ thin bread stick, 4 cm in diameter

3 For the Payoyo cheese base
2 g calcium gluconolactate (Gluco)
70 g mineral water
90 g cream, 35% fat
110 g Payoyo sheep's milk cheese
q.s. black pepper

4 For the alginate bath
500 g mineral water
2.5 g alginate (Algin)

5 For the Payoyo cheese spheres
q.s. Payoyo cheese base *(see point 3)*
q.s. alginate bath *(see point 4)*
1 kg mineral water
15 g salt

6 For the Payoyo cheese wedges
100 g Payoyo sheep's milk cheese (1 wedge 7 cm long x 5 cm wide)

7 For the toasted bread
¼ bread stick (the traditional *tourchon* bread stick 9 cm in diameter is recommended)

1 For the lemon jam
Peel half the lemons, leaving the segments, and leave the other half with the rind on, removing the top and bottom stem. Dice into cubes.
Put the diced lemon, sugar and glucose in a saucepan, and cook on a low heat until the lemon is candied. Store in a container in the fridge.

2 To prepare the bread
Cut the bread on the bias using a knife, into slices 2 cm thick. Some 10 similar slices are required. Arrange on a tray lined with parchment paper and bake at 120ºC for 10 min and, later, at 160ºC for 5 min. Cool to room temperature and store in a container in a cool and dry place.

3 For the Payoyo cheese base
Dissolve the Gluco in half the water. Mix the remaining water with the cream and bring to the boil. Remove the cheese rind and dice into cubes.
Put the cheese in the food processor and add the cream mixture and the water and Gluco mixture. Season with freshly ground black pepper as necessary and beat to a fine cream.
Pass through a fine sieve and cool in the fridge for 2 h.

4 For the alginate bath
Mix the water and the alginate in a mixer or food processor until fully dissolved, then strain.
Let it stand for 24 h in a bowl in the fridge to eliminate the accumulated air bubbles. Keep refrigerated.

5 For the Payoyo cheese spheres
Put the alginate bath in a container that allows a height of 8 cm.
Using a 15-ml, metal, semi-spherical spoon, form spheres with the Payoyo base and cook for 1 min in the alginate mixture. Rinse the sphere in water and store in the salt and water mixture. Set aside in the fridge.

6 For the Payoyo cheese wedges
Cut 4 wedges, 10 g each, and set aside in the fridge.

7 For the toasted bread
Freeze the bread for 30 min.
Slice the bread with a meat-slicing machine set at number 3 (40 similar slices will be obtained).
Arrange them on a baking tray lined with parchment paper and bake at 160ºC for 10 min. Cool to room temperature and store in a container in a cool and dry place.

Finishing and presentation

Using a slotted spoon, remove the Payoyo cheese sphere from the salted water, remove the excess water with a paper towel and place on top of a spoon for spheres.

On top of each sphere, put a dab of lemon jam and a crunchy slice of bread on top.

On another dish, place a wedge of cheese and a piece of toast.

Serve all together.

TOASTED STEAMED BRIOCHE WITH TRUFFLED CHEESE

X 4

1 For the brioche dough
250 g flour
75 g butter
10 g compressed fresh yeast
20 g sugar
80 g full-fat milk
90 g whole egg
5 g salt

2 For the brioche
q.s. brioche dough
(see point 1)

3 For the cheese mixture
170 g buffalo mozzarella
25 g buffalo mozzarella whey
70 g provolone

4 For the black truffle paste
10 g black truffle
(fresh or frozen)
10 g buffalo mozzarella whey

5 For the truffled cheese
135 g cheese mixture
(see point 3)
18 g black truffle paste
(see point 4)

6 For the truffled brioche
4 brioche *(see point 2)*
60 g truffled cheese
(see point 5)

1 For the brioche dough
Pour the flour into a kneading machine with the dough hook.
Soften the butter at room temperature.
Heat the milk to 37°C and add the sugar and yeast.
Run the kneading machine at minimum speed and gradually add the milk mixture to the flour.
Next, gradually add the butter and, finally, the beaten egg, also bit by bit.
Turn up the speed to number 2.
When the dough begins to have a smooth consistency, add the salt.
Knead for an additional 5 min and remove from the machine.
Set the dough aside wrapped in plastic wrap for 24 h in the fridge.

2 For the brioche
Divide the dough into 150-g portions and roll out manually into strips of dough 2 cm thick.
Using a knife, divide the dough into 17-g portions.
Roll the dough into balls and place on a tray lined with parchment paper. Allow the brioche dough to ferment for 50 or 60 min.
Cook the brioche in the oven at 94°C (in the case of a steam oven, set at 100% humidity and the fan at medium power) for 15 min.
Cool the brioche to room temperature and store in a container in the fridge.

3 For the cheese mixture
Mix the provolone cheese and the whey in a mixer.
Add the mozzarella and blend to a smooth cream.

4 For the black truffle paste
Blend the truffle and the whey to a paste in a mixer.

5 For the truffled cheese
Mix the cheese mixture and the black truffle paste. Set aside in a piping bag at room temperature.

6 For the truffled brioche
Remove the brioche from the fridge; 5 mm from the bottom make a 1.5-cm incision and remove the dough filling (a 15-g piece of brioche will remain).
Cut off the tip of a plastic piping bag leaving a 5-mm hole and fill the brioche through the incision with 15 g of the mixture. Check that the final weight of the filled brioche is 30 g.
Set aside in the fridge, covered to prevent a loss of moisture.

Finishing and presentation
Remove the brioche from the fridge 30 min before serving and let it stand at room temperature. Toast in a sandwich toaster with parchment paper on a medium heat until golden on both sides. Serve.

TALO CORN TORTILLA WITH SUCKLING PIG CONFIT, LIME ZEST AND CRACKLING PORK

X 4

1 For the *talo* corn tortilla dough
100 g cornflour (Maseca)
20 g wheat flour
q.s. fine salt
100 g hot water

2 For the crushed herb seasoning
16 g fresh oregano
20 g fresh thyme
300 g garlic
4 g bay leaf
12 g cumin seeds
q.s. salt
q.s. pepper

3 For the suckling pig confit
500 g suckling pig
1 kg pork fat
10 g fine salt
q.s. black pepper
c. s. crushed herb seasoning
(see point 2)

4 For the crisp pork skin
100 g pork skin *(see point 3)*

5 To shred the suckling pig confit
q.s. suckling pig confit
(see point 3)

Finishing and presentation
8 coriander sprouts
1 lime

❶ For the *talo* corn tortilla dough
See next page.

❷ For the crushed herb seasoning
Remove the oregano and thyme leaves. Crush the peeled garlic, bay leaves, cumin, oregano and thyme along with the salt and pepper in a mortar. Set aside.

❸ For the suckling pig confit
Cut the suckling pig into the following parts: head, ribcage, shoulder blade and hind leg. Remove the skin and set aside.
Season with salt and pepper and cover each part of the suckling pig with the crushed herb seasoning.
Melt the pork fat on the heat. Place the suckling pig ribcage and head in one container, and the shoulder blade and leg in another.
Cover the suckling pig with pork fat and parchment paper with a weight on top to prevent it from drying out.
Preheat the oven to 90°C and cook the head and ribcage for 4 h, and the shoulder blade and leg for 5 h. Remove and allow to cool to room temperature.

❹ For the crisp pork skin
Separate the skin from the suckling pig meat.
Put the skin on the grill, for the minimum amount of time for it to brown, and turn over.
Remove the skin from the grill and put in the oven to dry out for 1 h at 110°C between two racks covered with parchment paper.
When crisp, remove and allow to cool to room temperature.
Dice into 1 x 0.5 cm cubes and set aside in a container with a packet of silica gel.

❺ To shred the suckling pig
Remove the suckling pig from the fat and allow to drain.
Separate the meat from the rest of the skin. Make 2 x 1 cm strips and set aside in a container in the fridge.

Finishing and presentation
Pour off the pork fat to leave the crushed herb seasoning that will be used to dress the *talo*.
As the *talos* are cooking (*see point 6 on the next page*) prepare the suckling pig, placing it in a heat-resistant mesh basket immersed in the fat to sauté the suckling pig.
Finally, fill the *talo* with the suckling pig, dress with the crushed herb seasoning, and put 3 pieces of crisp pig skin on top, 2 coriander sprouts and sprinkle with a little grated lime zest.

Mix the cornflour, wheat flour and salt. Moisten the mixture with water.

1

Knead lightly to form a dough with a smooth consistency that is easy to knead by hand.

2

HOW TO PREPARE THE *TALOS*

There are few corn-based dishes. Internationally, Mexican tacos are well known. In Spain, however, there are also good examples of corn tortillas, such as *tortos*, very typical in the cuisine of Asturias, and *talos*, in the Basque Country, which are filled with the sautéd suckling pig in this recipe.

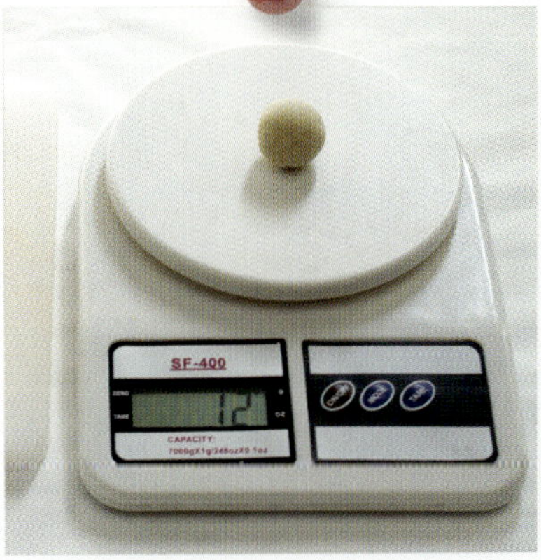

Measure out 12-g portions of dough and form balls of dough manually.

3

Put 4 balls of corn dough in a machine for rolling out Mexican tortillas.

4

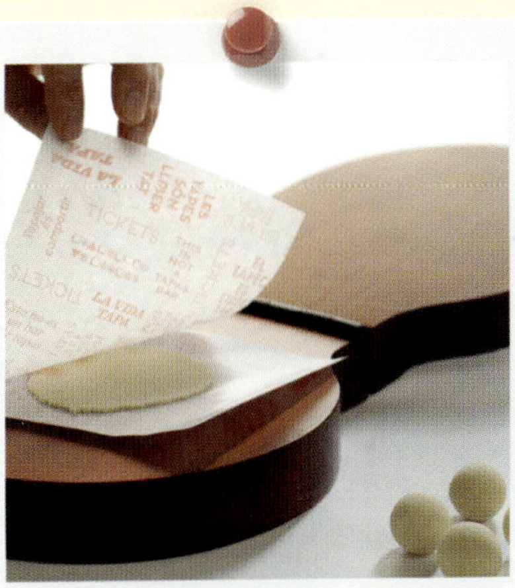

Place in the tortilla press between two pieces of parchment.

5

Make the *talos* as thin as possible and sear quickly on a grill at a high temperature.

6

ROASTED PORK RIBS WITH BARBECUE SAUCE

X 4

❶ For the barbecue sauce

4 g garlic
20 g onion
5 g olive oil, 0.4° acidity
5 g whiskey
90 g ketchup
30 g muscovado sugar
20 g apple vinegar
10 g Perrins sauce
10 g HP sauce
5 g liquid smoke
2 g Dijon mustard

❷ To roast the pork ribs

800 g pork ribs
q.s. fine salt
1.2 kg pork fat

Finishing and presentation

4 bamboo leaves (optional)

❶ For the barbecue sauce

Thinly slice the garlic and onion and sauté in a pan with oil until the onion is translucent.
Raise the temperature to a high heat, add the whiskey and reduce until it has evaporated.
Add the remaining ingredients and allow to boil for 5 min.
Blend in a mixer or food processor, then strain.
Cook for an additional 5 min for the sauce to acquire a more intense colour and set aside.

❷ To roast the pork ribs

Separate the ribs one by one.
Cut into pieces 10 cm long.
Season one by one and place in an ovenproof dish with the pork fat. Roast in the oven at 130°C for 2 h.
Make sure the ribs are tender and allow to cool to room temperature.
Drain in a colander. Set aside.

Finishing and presentation

Using a brush, baste the ribs with the barbecue sauce one by one and put in the oven (a charcoal oven is best) at a temperature of 250°C. Leave for 2 min until they caramelise.
Turn over and baste with the barbecue sauce and leave for an additional 2 min in the oven.
They can be served on a dish on top of a bamboo leaf.

SOT-L'Y-LAISSE SKEWER OF FREE-RANGE CHICKEN WITH MINI-SHIITAKE MUSHROOMS

X 4

❶ To clean the *sot-l'y-laisse*
20 chicken *sot-l'y-laisse*

❷ For the marinade
5 g roast chicken spices
60 g white wine
30 g olive oil, 0.4° acidity
5 g fine salt

❸ For the marinated *sot-l'y-laisse*
300 g clean *sot-l'y-laisse* *(see point 1)*
100 g marinade *(see point 2)*

❹ For the crushed herb seasoning
4 g fresh mint
6 g fresh oregano
20 g fresh parsley
q.s. fine salt
20 g lemon juice
80 g olive oil, 0.4° acidity

❺ To assemble the skewers
16 mini-shiitake mushrooms
20 marinated *sot-l'y-laisse* *(see point 3)*

❶ To clean the *sot-l'y-laisse*
Using a knife blade, remove the excess fat from the *sot-l'y-laisse*, as well as any bones.

❷ For the marinade
Mix all the ingredients together in a bowl with a whisk. Set aside.

❸ For the marinated *sot-l'y-laisse*
In a tall container, mix the clean *sot-l'y-laisse* and the chicken marinade.
Leave to marinade cold for 15 min.

❹ For the crushed herb seasoning
Finely chop the mint, oregano and parsley with a knife. Mix the herbs in a bowl with the salt, lemon juice and oil. Set aside.

❺ To assemble the skewers
Cut away the mini-shiitake stems.
Put on a skewer, interspersing 5 pieces of chicken *sot-l'y-laisse* with 4 mini-shiitake mushrooms (each skewer will weigh 100 g).

Finishing and presentation
Dress the skewers with the marinade and season the shiitake mushrooms with salt. Sear the skewers on the grill without overcooking them. Sprinkle with the crushed herb seasoning and serve.

FRIED POTATOES WITH RIB JUICE AND PORK SHOULDER

X 4

1 To fry the potatoes
520 g Mona Lisa potatoes
560 g olive oil, 0.4° acidity

2 For the rib juice
1.5 kg pork rib
8 g garlic
50 g onion
40 g red wine
400 g mineral water
q.s. salt

3 For the ham stock
100 g ham cuts
400 g ham bones
400 g mineral water

4 For the rib and ham gravy
90 g rib juice *(see point 2)*
80 g ham stock *(see point 3)*
20 g mineral water
10 g cornflour (Maizena)

5 To cut the cooked Iberian ham
500 g cooked Iberian ham

Finishing and presentation
5 g La Vera smoked paprika
5 g fine salt
5 g virgin olive oil

1 To fry the potatoes

Peel the potatoes.
Cut the potatoes into uneven 3-cm pieces.
Fry the potatoes in 160 g of oil in a deep-fat fryer at 130°C for 6 min.
Drain and put in a tall stainless steel container with the remaining oil, roasting at 180°C in a preheated oven, for 12 min. Lower the temperature to 130°C and continue cooking for an additional 12 min. Remove the potatoes from the oven and allow to stand at room temperature.

2 For the rib juice

In a frying pan, sear the chopped pork rib on all sides.
Add the crushed garlic cloves and sauté.
Add the julienned onion and sauté. Add salt as necessary.
Deglaze with red wine and reduce. Add the mineral water and allow to cook gently to extract the juices and to let the water evaporate gradually.

3 For the ham stock

Chop up the ham cuts and bones and allow to cook in water in a saucepan.
Cook on a low heat for 1 h and strain.
Strain the stock through paper towels, thereby obtaining a ham consommé.

4 For the rib and ham gravy

Put the rib juice and ham stock on the heat. Add the cornflour and water and stir until smooth. Add gradually to the boiling stock mixture and cook to the desired consistency. Set aside.

5 To cut the cooked Iberian ham

Remove the outer rind of the ham and leave it clean. Cut into quarters and set aside.

Finishing and presentation

Warm up the fried potatoes in the same oil when about to assemble the dish.
Cut the ham with a meat-slicing machine into 6 thin slices (60 g per person).
Arrange 6 drained and hot potatoes seasoned with salt on the dish, pour over the gravy and garnish each potato with the Iberian ham. Dress the ham and sprinkle over the paprika.
Place under the grill until the ham and its fat warm up.
Finish with a drizzle of virgin olive oil and serve.

GUIDE TO USING THIS BOOK

OR HOW TO MAKE TICKETS TAPAS AT HOME

Recipes from the Tickets restaurant featured in this book are accessible for chefs of any nature, from cooking enthusiasts to catering professionals.

If, when leafing through the book, any reader feels they shall never be able to reproduce the cuisine at Tickets, they are mistaken. Among the 55 recipes contained herein, are recipes of varying degrees of difficulty. Begin with the simplest recipes (*) and, once you reap your first successes, you will no doubt dare to prepare more complicated tapas.

In any case, what follows is a set of tips and tricks to help you put these dishes into practice:

1. The use of abbreviations is limited. In addition to the various units of weight, volume and time, the reader will come across "q.s." (sufficient quantity). Generally speaking, it refers to the amount of salt or oil required for a dish, in which the chef's taste also comes into play.

2. Vacuum sealing machines are widely used in professional kitchens today. Besides being used to prolong products' shelf life, whether raw or semi-processed items, a vacuum-sealing machine is employed to accelerate culinary processes. In this regard, if you do not have a vacuum-sealing machine, simply place the ingredients in an airtight container and set the ingredients aside in the fridge for 24 hours (*see page 23*, for instance).

3. Vacuum sealing is also used for cooking at low temperatures, known as "sous-vide" cooking. The food is placed in heat-resistant bags, the air is removed and they are sealed and cooked in a Roner (this is the name of the appliance though it is a brand) at a temperature that ranges between 5 and 100ºC. With this type of cooking, the food's properties are better conserved, moisture is retained and the shelf life is extended. Should you not have a Roner, once vacuum packed, the food can be cooked at a low temperature in a tall container filled with water, controlling the temperature with an oven thermometer. If you do not have vacuum bags either, you can use plastic wrap. For example, if you wish to cook a leg of lamb at a low temperature, it is first browned in a frying pan with oil. Then it is placed in an oven tray, the container is covered with plastic wrap and cooked in the oven at 75ºC for 12 h. If your oven is not a steam oven, placing the container in a saucepan filled with water to generate moisture is recommended.

   Furthermore, to cook bivalve molluscs, such as mussels (*see page 122*) or razor clams (*see pages 93 and 96*), instead of sous-vide cooking, the shellfish can be submerged in salted water and boiled until it opens.

4 In some dishes, such as the oyster with its pearl and sea lettuce water (*see page 46*), a smoking gun is used. It is a highly useful tool that can be purchased from €50 in specialised kitchen product establishments such as Solé Graells (also available online: solegraells.com).

5 A pasta machine appears in recipes such as the mini-airbags filled with Manchego cheese foam (*see page 34*). Besides being used for this dish, it is a utensil that will be put to good use when making homemade pasta. It can be purchased in hypermarkets and specialty stores.

6 In some recipes (*see cod fritters on page 30*), the ingredients are dried, such as parsley, with a dehydrator. If you do not have this appliance, the procedure can be performed in an oven that heats to a temperature lower than 60 °C. The drying time will be the same in both devices.

7 Alginate, calcium salt, agar and xanthan, among others, are basic ingredients in Tickets cuisine, and that I began to use at elBulli. Thanks to these products, our signature techniques can be replicated such as hot jellies, airs, spherifications, etc. For more in-depth details regarding these products, please see albertyferranadria.com. They are available for purchase in speciality stores such as Solé Graells, and also on its website: www.solegraells.com

8 Another feature of Tickets cuisine is the use of Asian ingredients, such as kombu, granulated dashi and Korean soy sauce. You will be able to find them in Asian food stores. dongfang.es and www.iberochina.com offer a large selection of products online.

9 Many people ask me where and when I buy the best oysters. Trust your regular suppliers. As far as the season is concerned, those originating from the Ebro Delta and Galicia are in their prime, as is traditionally claimed, in the months that contain the letter "r". In summer, I also usually buy oysters imported from France and Ireland.

10 The brands quoted herein are simply my recommendations, those that I consider best for preparing these dishes. However, they are by no means essential.

The author

RECIPE INDEX

In alphabetical order and level of preparation difficulty

TICKETS TIPS

OTHER DISHES THAT APPEAR IN THE BOOK

THE TEAM AT TICKETS

TICKETS

TICKETS' collaborators

Estrella Damm · Coca-Cola · Flores Valles cocinas profesionales · Moët & Chandon Champagne

Cooked in Barcelona · Luis Cañas · Joselito · Lavazza · Lustau · Roca · SAGA Creacions Gràfiques, S.A.

Juvé y Camps · Pazo de Señorans · Torelló Cava · Riedel · Sighore · nanimarquina

LA VIDA TAPA

EL TAPEO ES LLIBER TAD

Tapejar és compartir

TICKETS

Això no és pas un bar de tapes

TAPEAR ES COMPARTIR

LES TAPES SÓN LLIBER TAT

Tapas are free dom

LA VIDA TAPA

THIS IS NOT A TAPAS BAR

TAPEJAR ÉS COMPARTIR

La vida tapa

TICKETS

TAPAS ARE FREE DOM

THIS IS NOT A TAPAS BAR

LES TAPES SÓN LLIBER TAT

Això no és pas un bar de tapes

Tapear es compartir

EL TAPEO ES LLIBER TAD

La vida tapa

EL TAPEO ES LLIBER TAD

Esto no es un bar de tapas

LA VIDA TAPA

Això no és pas un bar de tapes

TICKETS

TAPAS ARE FREE DOM

THIS IS NOT A TAPAS BAR

LES TAPES SÓN LLIBER TAT

LA VIDA TAPA

Tapear es compartir

LES TAPES SÓN LLIBER TAT

THIS IS NOT A TAPAS BAR

LA VIDA TAPA

TAPAS ARE FREE DOM

TICKETS

LA VIDA TAPA

Tapejar és compartir

Esto no es un bar de tapas

EL TAPEO ES LLIBER TAD

LA VIDA TAPA